The power of God in Ray Johnston's life is undeniable. In his book, This Changes Everything, Johnston shows us how Christ's resurrection power can transform our lives.

Craig Groeschel, Senior Pastor of LifeChurch.tv
Author of *Weird, Because Normal Isn't Working*

Nothing will impact your life more thoroughly than your understanding of the resurrection story of Jesus Christ. As my good friend Ray Johnston so aptly shows us, the resurrection account of Jesus Christ—as clearly taught in the Bible—truly does change everything. I have experienced it in my life and witnessed it in the lives of hundreds of thousands of others. I challenge you to read this book, share it with your friends, and contemplate how one dramatic event 2,000 years ago has changed the course of history for each one of us.

Luis Palau, World Evangelist

Not only has Ray Johnston been one of my closest friends and an amazing mentor to me for the last ten years, but I've also seen firsthand his incredible gift as a communicator, leader, and author. His desire for both believers *and* the lost to know the risen Christ is unmatched. Ray's passion for seeing lives transformed is the foundation of *This Changes Everything*. He clearly unpacks the resurrection story of Jesus Christ and shows how this one event has changed everything, for everyone, forever. This is absolutely a must read for anyone!

Lincoln Brewster, Some random dude Ray met one day and paid handsome sums of m̶o̶ ̶ ̶ ̶ ̶ ̶ ̶ ̶ ̶ ̶ ̶ ̶ ̶ things about him
Worship Pastor of Bayside Church

D0181463

This Changes Everything

This Changes Everything

unleashing the power of the resurrection in your life

ray johnston

IVP Books

An imprint of InterVarsity Press
Downers Grove, Illinois

InterVarsity Press
P.O. Box 1400, Downers Grove, IL 60515-1426
World Wide Web: www.ivpress.com
E-mail: email@ivpress.com

InterVarsity Press® is the book-publishing division of InterVarsity Christian Fellowship/USA®, a movement of students and faculty active on campus at hundreds of universities, colleges and schools of nursing in the United States of America, and a member movement of the International Fellowship of Evangelical Students. For information about local and regional activities, write Public Relations Dept., InterVarsity Christian Fellowship/USA, 6400 Schroeder Rd., P.O. Box 7895, Madison, WI 53707-7895, or visit the IVCF website at <www.intervarsity.org>.

Originally published by Biblica.

ISBN 978-0-8308-5768-5

Printed in the United States of America ∞

Cataloging-in-Publication Data is available through the Library of Congress.

| **P** | 16 | 15 | 14 | 13 | 12 | 11 | 10 | 9 | 8 | 7 | 6 | 5 | 4 | 3 |
| **Y** | 25 | 24 | 23 | 22 | 21 | 20 | 19 | 18 | 17 | 16 | 15 | 14 | 13 |

Dedication

To my kids:
Mark, Scott, Christy, and Leslie

You invaded our lives, and for twenty-one years your soccer, volleyball, basketball, homework, guitars (and more guitars), hamsters, stray cats, small fish, big horses, lost dogs, found Christmas scavenger presents, vacations, broken bones, trampolines, and Kings games have caused laughter to echo off our walls. Out of all the kids in the world, Mom and I would choose you! We are so proud of the young men and women you have become. You have always been fun to hang out with and a joy to parent. I love you.

—Dad

Acknowledgments

A friend of mine tells a joke about a man who entered his donkey in the Kentucky Derby. When questioned about this, the man replied, "Oh, I don't expect him to win, but I thought the association would do him good."

During this project, I have enjoyed the association of some world-class people. I would like to express my appreciation to a few of them.

To project coordinator, Sarah Bentley: Your energy, class, and positive spirit consistently turn work into fun. Your laughter and joy are contagious. You are England's best export to America. I'll thank the queen next time I see her.

To my cowriter, Bob Smietana: You are a talented writer, thinker, and editor. And you consistently went the extra mile for this project. Thanks for everything.

To Darlene Anderson and Candy Brown: Your faithfulness to the cause of Christ and your loyalty to me and to Bayside continue to inspire the community and me.

To Paul Carroll: Your editing brilliance is coupled with a genuine love for God and people. You have the gift of making everything and everyone better.

To my longtime assistant, Cindy Uhler: I am still not sure how you get it all done. Bayside would not be at the level it is without you. Neither would I.

To Lincoln Brewster: Knowing you are leading worship makes me break the speed limit driving to church. You are the best!

To David Durham, Tim Chambers, Kerry Shearer, and John Volinsky: Four guys who make the impossible happen regularly. The care and excellence you bring honor God.

To Phil Sommerville, Jeri Mann, Patty Lauterjung, and Denise Belden: Your writing, thoughts, and support have been invaluable.

To the Bayside staff: I am convinced that God looked down and said, "I'd better surround Ray with really good people." He has. No pastor has had the privilege of working with a finer group of people.

To the Bayside leadership team: I am grateful for your commitment to Christ, your care and concern for my family and me, and your diligent oversight of the ministries of our family of churches.

To my executive assistant, Donna Bostwick: It's wonderful for Carol and me to have a person in our lives who not only can run the universe but is also someone we like to hang out with. Thanks for keeping me and everything else on track.

And to my wife, Carol: I will be forever grateful that God allowed me to marry my best friend. Thanks for everything!

Contents

Foreword

When I was twenty-one years old, a group of Christians challenged me to discredit the claims of Christianity. Having discounted them all my life, I figured the challenge would be easy. After all, I thought, one needed to check his brains at the door of most churches. Applying a little reason should make the claims disappear.

I decided the fastest way to do away with the claims of the Christian faith would be to discredit the resurrection of Jesus Christ. I began there. The more I studied, however, the more I uncovered overwhelming historical evidence for the existence of Christ and for his resurrection. That discovery not only led me to a personal relationship with Jesus Christ but it also took me on a lifelong journey, writing and speaking around the world about the resurrection and its impact on our lives.

In *This Changes Everything,* Ray Johnston explores thirty-one practical ways the resurrection changed the lives of the early Christians and can transform us today. You will be challenged as you discover how the truth of the resurrection can change your life.

It is my prayer that this book will help you experience the power and presence of God. You'll find, as I did, there is no better way to live.

—Josh McDowell

Introduction

Something Happened in That Room

I grew up in a family of skeptics. We doubted everything. Reading books such as *Inherit the Wind* (drawn from the 1925 "Scopes Monkey Trial"), I assumed there was little evidence for the existence of God and even less for the validity of the Christian faith. My spiritual cynicism was so hardened I actually talked a friend out of becoming a Christian.

Finally, I took an honest look at the evidence (summarized in chapter 32). After a six-month investigation, I found, much to my surprise, that the evidence for the historical reliability of Jesus' resurrection was compelling. I completely lost my lack of faith.

Even more to my surprise, I discovered that I wasn't just making an intellectual decision. I was also unleashing in my life the kind of transforming power we're all striving to find. One of my favorite stories explains the power of Christ's resurrection, available and waiting for our discovery and use.

On their honeymoon, Scott and Leslie Holst arrived at a fancy hotel in the wee hours of the morning. They excitedly looked forward to spending their first night together in a luxurious bed in the hotel's bridal suite. When they got to their room, they found a sofa, chair, and table—but no bed. After several minutes, they discovered the sofa was a hide-a-bed. They spent a fitful night tossing and turning on a lumpy mattress with sagging springs.

Their honeymoon night ruined, Scott stormed down the next morning to the front desk and gave the clerk a tongue-lashing.

"There must be some mistake," the clerk said, after checking the Holst's reservation. "Didn't you open the door to the bedroom?"

Scott went back up to the room, opened the door he thought led to a closet, and discovered the bedroom to the bridal suite. Inside was a king-sized bed covered with fruit baskets, boxes of chocolates, and a dozen red roses. Completely available, yet totally unused!

Some doors are too important to leave closed. This book is an invitation to open the door to the implications of Christ's resurrection and its power in your life.

The early Christians spent the first Easter Sunday behind locked doors. They huddled together, fearing for their lives. Jesus had just been killed, and they thought they were next. They walked into that room defeated. But they walked out dynamic. They walked into that room crushed. They walked out confident. They walked in having a pity party. They walked out ready to take on the world. They walked into that room paralyzed by fear. They walked out filled with faith. Something happened in that room.

What happened? That's what this book is about. Join me for the next thirty-two chapters and you too can experience the same transformation the disciples underwent that first Easter.

Now, I should note that the New Testament doesn't confine the basis of our transformation to Jesus' resurrection apart from his incarnation, life, death, and ascension. What we sometimes refer to as "the work of Christ" includes this whole package. One Scripture might trumpet one of these aspects and the benefits it brings, while a different text heralds another.

The apostle Paul was likely quoting one of the church's first hymns when he wrote the following about Jesus Christ:

> *He appeared in the flesh,*
> *was vindicated by the Spirit,*
> *was seen by angels,*
> *was preached among the nations,*
> *was believed on in the world,*
> *was taken up in glory.* 1 Timothy 3:16

The Holy Spirit "vindicated" Jesus in a number of ways, including authenticating that Jesus' words were from God and that his miracles were done by God's power. But the most significant way the Spirit vindicated Christ was by raising him from the dead—demonstrating that he was indeed God's Son.

So while we cannot technically separate Christ's resurrection from his incarnation, death, and ascension, it's fitting that we place particular emphasis in this study on his resurrection.

I hope you'll find this book so compelling that you'll want to read it in one sitting. I suggest, however, that you instead take it one chapter at a time. Each chapter has one or two reflection questions for you to think about. As you read and reflect on this book, I pray you'll experience the same power I've discovered.

Now, open the door and unleash the power of Jesus' resurrection in your life.

chapter 1

Because of Jesus and his resurrection . . .

You Can Develop a Confident Faith

> *Jesus replied, "Truly I tell you, if you have faith*
> *and do not doubt, not only can you do what*
> *was done to the fig tree, but also you can say to*
> *this mountain, 'Go, throw yourself into the sea,'*
> *and it will be done."* Matthew 21:21

A story is told about a pastor in northern Wisconsin. The lack of pastors in the area meant he often traveled to rural communities to conduct funerals. He usually traveled with the undertaker, riding in the hearse. One day, on the way home from a funeral, the exhausted pastor decided to take a nap. Since they were in a hearse, he lay down in the back.

In time, the hearse ran low on fuel, so the undertaker pulled into a gas station. (This was back in the day when you didn't have to pump your own gas.) As the attendant filled the tank, he noticed a body stretched out in the back.

Just as the freaked out attendant finished his task, the pastor suddenly woke up, opened his eyes, knocked on the window, and waved at the attendant. The minister said in his whole life he'd never seen anybody run so fast!

When people see life where they are expecting death—there is a reaction!

None of the disciples expected life on Easter Sunday, especially not one of my favorite people in the Bible, Thomas. He's gotten a bad rap in the church. We call him "Doubting Thomas" and mock his lack of faith. But I, having grown up in a "show-me-the-evidence" family, respect Thomas for his honesty.

Put yourself in his shoes for a minute. He wasn't with the other disciples when Jesus first appeared to them on Easter. So, when they told him, "We have seen the Lord," Thomas found it a little hard to swallow. "Unless I see the nail marks in his hands and put my finger where the nails were, and put my hand into his side," he said, "I will not believe" (John 20:25).

Here's what Thomas was really saying: "I followed Jesus for three years. I heard his words and saw his miracles. I believed in him. But now he's dead. And I will not believe he's alive until I see him with my own eyes." Thomas wasn't about to settle for a secondhand faith and a secondhand God. He wanted a faith with reasons, one that based its foundation on fact. Thomas was saying he would follow Jesus if, and only if, he was convinced Jesus was alive!

For Thomas, and those of us like him, proof of the resurrection is essential. After all, who needs a dead Savior?

A week later, Thomas got what he asked for. Jesus appeared to the disciples. "Put your finger here; see my hands," Jesus told Thomas. "Reach out your hand and put it into my side. Stop doubting and believe" (John 20:27).

Jesus once told his disciples that if they had faith and did not doubt, they would be able to move mountains. After the resurrection, that's exactly what the disciples did. They traveled the world, testifying that Jesus had risen from the grave. Within three hundred years, even the Roman emperor would kneel to worship Jesus.

Thomas put aside his doubt and lived for Jesus. He knew that his faith in Christ was not in vain.

The same cannot be said for famed author and playwright George Bernard Shaw. In Shaw's play "Too True to Be Good," one character declares the following, which some have taken to be Shaw's own view:

> The science I pinned my faith to is bankrupt: its tales were more foolish than all the miracles of the priests, its cruelties more horrible than all the atrocities of the Inquisition. Its spread of enlightenment has been a spread of cancer: its counsels that were to have established the millennium have led straight to European suicide. And I—I who believed in it as no religious fanatic has ever believed in his superstition! For its sake I helped

to destroy the faith of millions of worshippers in the temples of a thousand creeds. And now look at me and behold the supreme tragedy of the atheist who has lost his faith—his faith in atheism, for which more martyrs have perished than for all the creeds put together.[1]

Stop doubting and believe.

For reflection . . .

How do you feel about "Doubting Thomas"? Does he remind you of yourself in some ways?

chapter 2

Because of Jesus and his resurrection . . .

You Can Receive Eternal Life

*For it is by grace you have been saved, through
faith—and this is not from yourselves, it is the
gift of God—not by works, so that no one can
boast.* Ephesians 2:8–9

A veteran Sunday school teacher tells the following
story.

> "If I sell my house and my car, have a big
> garage sale, and give all my money to the
> church, will that get me into heaven?" I asked
> the children in my Sunday school class.
>
> "No!" the children all answered.
>
> "If I clean the church every day, mow the
> yard, and keep everything neat and tidy, will
> that get me into heaven?"
>
> The answer again was, "No!"
>
> "Well, then, if I treat animals kindly, give
> candy to all the children, and love my wife,
> will that get me into heaven?"

Again they all answered, "No!"

"Well," I continued, "then how can I get into heaven?"

A five-year-old boy shouted out, "You gotta be dead!"

Here's the answer the Sunday school teacher was looking for: *Heaven is a gift that must be received.*

"For God so loved the world that he gave his one and only Son, that whoever believes in him shall not perish but have eternal life. For God did not send his Son into the world to condemn the world, but to save the world through him" (John 3:16–17). These words couldn't be clearer. Jesus didn't come to condemn us—he came to save us. That's the good news! Eternal life is a gift, but it must be received.

Perhaps this story will help.

> Two baseball teams were deadlocked in a championship game. It was the bottom of the ninth inning, two runners out. The batter hit a shot that ricocheted off the center-field wall. He sped around first base, second, and third— then he raced for home plate. With the crowd screaming and the relay throw coming, he slid across home plate just before the catcher could make the tag. The crowd went nuts, and the batter's team sprinted onto the field to celebrate. But, to everyone's shock, the umpire shouted, "You're out!"

Pandemonium ensued. The crowd began booing. The manager went berserk.

When the umpire finally got a word in edgewise, he announced, "He's not out because he got tagged at home. He's out because *he missed first base!*"

Establishing a relationship with God is like touching first base. It couldn't be more important. I can attend church, serve on a dozen committees, own the biggest Bible on the block, and memorize the Ten Commandments—but without a relationship with Christ, someday I will be called out at home plate.

This isn't about religion. God doesn't care if you're Catholic, Baptist, Presbyterian, or have no religious background. God is interested in having a relationship with you. He wants you to know his Son, Jesus Christ.

For reflection . . .

Have you touched first base? Have you said yes to Jesus Christ? Have you told God that you want to know him, that you want to be part of his family?

All you need to do is tell God that you need him, that you need his forgiveness, his power, and his presence in your life. Why not take that first step by praying the Easter Prayer on the following page?

You Can Receive Eternal Life

An Easter Prayer

> Dear God, thank you for sending your Son,
>   Jesus Christ, to earth.
> Jesus, I believe that you are who you said you are
>   and that you proved it by rising from the dead.
> I want to get to know you personally.
> Thank you, Jesus, for dying for me and
>   forgiving all my sins.
> Please forgive me for all my sins and come
>   into my life.
> I receive you as my Lord and Savior.
> Holy Spirit, change me into the new creation you
>   want me to be.
> Thank you for your free gift of eternal life.
> Amen.

chapter 3

Because of Jesus and his resurrection . . .

You Can Overcome the Odds

*I am still confident of this: I will see the
goodness of the LORD in the land of the living.*
Psalm 27:13

On July 18, 1929, boxer James J. Braddock stepped
into the ring at New York's Yankee Stadium for the biggest
fight of his life. Just twenty-four years old, Braddock was
a rising star in the ranks of professional boxers. Now he
was fighting for the light heavyweight championship of
the world. But Tommy Loughran, the reigning champion,
had studied Braddock's boxing style and was prepared for
his powerful right arm. Loughran's strategy of ducking and
dodging Braddock's punches was successful. Loughran won
the bout in a fifteen-round decision.

Braddock lost more than a boxing match that night.
His confidence was shot. To make matters worse, less than
two months later, the stock market crashed and he lost
everything. Though he had fractured his right hand in the
ring, Braddock kept boxing in order to put food on his

family's table during the Great Depression. He lost twenty times over his next thirty-three fights. His boxing license was suspended due to his poor performances, and he had to accept government charity to feed his family.

Then, in 1934, Braddock got a lucky break when he was a last-minute substitute in a match against heavyweight "Corn" Griffin, the number two contender in the world. To everyone's surprise, even his own, Braddock knocked Griffin out. After years of hard luck, he had his confidence back. As portrayed in the film *Cinderella Man,* Braddock would eventually become heavyweight champion of the world, defeating Max Baer despite being a ten-to-one underdog. As James Braddock demonstrated, there is no substitute for confidence.

The first words Jesus spoke to the disciples after his resurrection were these: "Peace be with you!" Because of Jesus' resurrection, we too can live with confidence. Nothing will raise your expectations, give hope, and restore relationships like having confident faith in Jesus Christ.

Notice the impact of faith:

Faith in God's *presence* gives me *peace!*

> *Do not be anxious about anything, but in every situation, by prayer and petition, with thanksgiving, present your requests to God. And the peace of God, which transcends all understanding, will guard your hearts and your minds in Christ Jesus.*
> Philippians 4:6–7

Faith in God's *call* gives me *purpose!*

> *For we are God's handiwork, created in Christ Jesus to do good works, which God prepared in advance for us to do.* Ephesians 2:10

Faith in God's *Word* gives me *direction!*

> *All Scripture is God-breathed and is useful for teaching, rebuking, correcting and training in righteousness, so that the servant of God may be thoroughly equipped for every good work.* 2 Timothy 3:16–17

Faith in God's *power* gives me *confidence!*

> *For I am confident of this very thing, that He who began a good work in you will perfect it until the day of Christ Jesus.* Philippians 1:6, NASB

A pastor friend shared with me some revealing observations he's made about the impact of confidence. He asked people, "If nothing was different in your life except for one thing— you were confident—how different would your life be?" My friend found that people with a high level of confidence are more satisfied, more willing to help others in need, physically healthier, more productive, and less affected by stress than are people with low confidence. Confident people are also more likely to see God as loving, caring, and forgiving.

We can be confident in this, David tells us in Psalm 27:13: we will see "the goodness of the LORD in the land of the living." The "land of the living" refers to this life. Though we will experience God's goodness in unfathomable ways in heaven, we don't have to wait until then to be confident in his benevolent presence.

For reflection . . .

Recall a time in your life when the odds were against you. How did God help you overcome those odds?

How has Christ's resurrection helped you live with confidence? In what area do you need to tap into that power more?

chapter 4

Because of Jesus and his resurrection . . .

You Can Discover That You Matter to God

For God so loved the world that he gave his one and only Son, that whoever believes in him shall not perish but have eternal life. John 3:16

Jesus said to her, "Mary." John 20:16

Utter despair and hopelessness. That's the picture of Mary on Easter Sunday. Her whole world had crumbled when Jesus was killed. She went to the tomb early that morning to follow Jewish customs by anointing Jesus' body with spices. At least she could pay her last respects to him.

When Mary got to the tomb, however, Jesus' body was gone. She could only stand outside the tomb and weep. In her despondency, Mary didn't recognize Jesus standing beside her. She thought he was the gardener.

"Sir," she said, "if you have carried him away, tell me where you have put him, and I will get him" (John 20:15).

Jesus spoke one word to her, a word that broke through all the discouragement. One word that lifted her spirit, turned her sorrow to joy, and changed forever the trajectory of her life. One simple word: "Mary." The moment she heard Jesus say her name, Mary realized he was alive. And he knew her name.

To people down through the ages, that is the message of Easter. *Jesus Christ is alive, and he knows your name.* You matter to God more than you will ever know. He created you. He watched you being formed in your mother's womb. He watched you take your first breath. God knows every heartache, every hurt, and every failure you have experienced. And, he loves you so much that he sent his Son to the world two thousand years ago to give his life for you.

A friend of mine, René Schlaepfer, tells the following story about Dave Roever, a man who experienced the power of unconditional love—in his case, as a gift from another human being.

> While serving in Vietnam, Dave suffered burns over 90 percent of his body when a phosphorus grenade he was about to throw exploded in his hand. The burns left him horribly disfigured and put him in the hospital for fourteen months. He was sent home and treated in a burn unit in a US hospital. Knowing how he looked, Dave felt that he was worthless to anyone and had no future.

Dave shared his hospital room with another soldier who had also been badly burned. One day this man's wife came to visit him. While she was there, she took off her wedding ring, put it on the nightstand, and said, "I'm so sorry, but there's no way I could live with you now. We are over." With that, she walked out the door.

Dave remembers that his roommate wept and shook for hours. And within two days, the young soldier was dead.

Three days later, Dave's wife, Brenda, came to visit him. In light of what had happened with his roommate, Dave had been dreading her visit. Charred black from the waist up, Dave steeled himself for Brenda's reaction as she approached him. But Brenda, a committed believer who had a great sense of humor, bent down and kissed Dave's disfigured face and quipped, "Frankly, Dave, in some ways, this is an improvement!"

Then Brenda smiled and said, "Honey, I love you. I'll always love you. We are going to get you on your feet and out of here." Within a matter of weeks, Dave had recovered enough to be released from the hospital.[1]

Today the risen Jesus speaks very similar words to you. "I love you. I will always love you. I know your name. I will never let you go."

For reflection . . .

> Though Jesus was standing right next to Mary, she didn't recognize him—until he called her name. Do you have a story about how God got your attention?
>
> What are the implications for our lives when we discover that we matter to God?

chapter 5

Because of Jesus and his resurrection . . .

You Can Experience Complete Transformation

I want to know Christ—yes, to know the power of his resurrection and participation in his sufferings, becoming like him in his death.
Philippians 3:10

John and Monica Kubena were in dire straits. A combination of financial difficulties and health problems with their twin daughters, Tara and Sara, who both had leukemia, had brought John and Monica to their knees. After treatment, the girls' cancer had gone into remission. But Tara's leukemia, unfortunately, had returned. A bone marrow transplant helped, but the Kubena's cramped home was no place for a sick child. Even the slightest infection could be fatal for Tara, so she had to be separated from the rest of the family. The house was too old and too small to keep her safe.

Hope came in the form of hundreds of crewmembers and volunteers from ABC's television show *Extreme Makeover: Home Edition*. In one week, the Kubena's small trailer was demolished, and a 4,200-square-foot home, with all the space the family of six needed, was built in its place.

Every week, millions of people tune in to *Extreme Makeover: Home Edition*. The show's executive producer, Tom Forman, explains why. "It's a fairy tale, a guaranteed happy ending. . . . There's just something very appealing doing good things for people who desperately need it."[1]

The families on the show experience total transformation—from pain and struggle to hope and joy, all in one week's time.

Easter promises transformation. The same power that raised Christ from the dead was unleashed in the lives of his followers and changed them forever. The apostle John described the transformation that took place because Jesus rose from the dead. The disciples were confused and filled with fear, but when the risen Christ appeared to them, they were filled with peace, hope, and joy (John 20:19–20).

Peter is the best example of this transformation. When Jesus was arrested, all the other disciples ran for their lives. Not Peter. He followed the crowd that had arrested Jesus, wanting to know Jesus' fate. But a servant girl noticed Peter and accused him of being a friend of Jesus. Others chimed in, recognizing Peter as a disciple. "I don't know the man!" Peter said, before running off in shame.

After the resurrection, however, the same Peter—who was afraid to admit to a lowly servant that he followed Jesus—stood before a huge crowd in Jerusalem and declared the story of the resurrection. Thousands decided to follow Jesus because of Peter's message. Talk about transformation!

The big question is, How can *we* be transformed by the power of Easter? Where do we find the strength to live as the disciples lived?

According to the apostle Paul, another early Christian whose life was turned upside down by the resurrection, the key to transformation is changing the way you think: "Do not conform to the pattern of this world," he wrote, "but be transformed by the renewing of your mind" (Romans 12:2).

John Maxwell, one of my mentors, says transformation comes in six stages:

1. When you change your thinking, you change your beliefs.
2. When you change your beliefs, you change your expectations.
3. When you change your expectations, you change your attitude.
4. When you change your attitude, you change your behavior.
5. When you change your behavior, you change your performance.
6. When you change your performance, you change your life![2]

Need an extreme makeover? It all starts with the power of Christ's resurrection!

For reflection . . .

What noticeable changes in your life have you experienced since you received Jesus Christ into your life? What difference has it made? Have your family and friends noticed?

Which of the six stages John Maxwell identifies most clearly describes where you are in transformation?

chapter 6

Because of Jesus and his resurrection . . .
You Can Live with God's Power

*Those who hope in the LORD will renew their
strength. They will soar on wings like eagles;
they will run and not grow weary, they will
walk and not be faint.* Isaiah 40:31

Perhaps clicking through the TV channels, looking
for something to watch, you've come across the "World's
Strongest Man" competition. These guys, weighing 300-
plus pounds, do all kinds of incredible things, such as
lifting giant logs, carrying 400-pound stones, and pulling
transport trucks—each trying to prove he is the world's
strongest man.

That kind of strength is impressive, but it doesn't match
the power that Jesus demonstrated. People flocked to him
because they saw him heal with a touch. They saw blind
people gain their sight, paralyzed people walk, and lepers
cleansed. Once, in the middle of a raging storm, Jesus even
spoke to the wind and waves, and the furious storm calmed
completely.

When Jesus stretched out his arms and hung on the cross, the crowds watching him die thought they were seeing weakness. They were wrong. They were witnessing the power of God as it had never before been displayed. Then, on Easter Sunday, Jesus burst out of the grave, conquering even death itself. And he offers that same power to each of us today.

The power that defeated death can give you the power to live life. If God could raise Jesus from the dead, he can raise a dead marriage. He can raise a dead career. He can raise a dead dream. He can give you strength to keep going when you feel that you can't take another step. And, at the end of your life, God will throw his arms around you and welcome you into his presence. That's the power of Easter.

The Bible tells us that we can experience the power of the resurrection. God "is able to do immeasurably more than all we ask or imagine, according to his power that is at work within us" (Ephesians 3:20). This verse says that the greatest power ever demonstrated on earth is available to every person on earth.

Recently, I heard a story that shows what it's like to live without that kind of power.

> A farmer had some trees to clear, so he went out to buy a new chainsaw. The salesperson sold him a saw guaranteed to cut down fifteen trees in one day. A week later, the unhappy farmer brought the saw back to the store and demanded to see the sales clerk. The farmer wanted his money back; he had worked all week and cut down only

three trees. "You sold me a piece of junk," he told the clerk.

The sales clerk apologized and asked to look at the saw. He pulled the cord, and the chainsaw started right up, with the familiar "Bzzzz" sound.

"Hey," demanded the startled farmer, "what's that noise?"

How many of us do like that farmer, trying to live by our own strength, never knowing the power we could have—if we would only ask?

For reflection . . .

How did Jesus demonstrate power through his life? Through his death? Through his resurrection?

In what ways do you feel the need to tap into God's power for your life?

chapter 7

Because of Jesus and his resurrection . . .

You Can Trust the Bible

> *For what I received I passed on to you as of*
> *first importance: that Christ died for our sins*
> *according to the Scriptures, that he was buried,*
> *that he was raised on the third day according to*
> *the Scriptures.* 1 Corinthians 15:3–4

Years ago when I spoke at a large youth convention in Southern California, a high school sophomore came to me during a break. "Dude," he said in typical Valley-speak, "You're an awesome speaker."

"Thanks, Dude," I responded. "You're an awesome listener."

Then he said, "Dude, there's only one problem. The Bible you're talking about isn't true! It's full of errors and stuff."

"Bummer," I said. "Looks like I'm going to have to get a new job. But before I quit, let me ask you, Which parts of the Bible aren't true?"

"I don't know," he admitted.

"And which errors are you talking about?"

Same answer. "I don't know."

Finally, I asked, "Have you ever read the Bible?"

You can probably guess his answer. "Nope," he said.

Unfortunately, my young friend isn't alone. Many people assume the Bible isn't accurate or authoritative. They're often unaware of the claims of Christ and the compelling evidence for trusting the Bible.

Here are a few things you may not know about the Bible.

The Bible is unique in its circulation.

It is the most widely read book in history. Find me another book that's been at the top of the bestseller list for four hundred years!

The Bible is unique in its translation.

Even though the New Testament has already been translated into more than 1,650 languages, a literal army of translators works today to make the Scriptures available to still more people.

The Bible is unique in its durability.

It has survived bans and burnings, ridicule and criticism. The Bible has outlived all of its cruelest opponents.

The Bible is unique in its impact.

Millions of people credit the Bible for transforming their lives; altering their view of the world; changing their relationships, their values, and their view of eternity.

The Bible is unique in its historical reliability.
In his book *The New Evidence That Demands a Verdict*, Josh McDowell writes, "After trying to shatter the historicity and validity of the Scripture, I came to the conclusion that it is historically trustworthy. If one discards the Bible as being unreliable, then one must discard almost all literature of antiquity."[1]

The apostle Paul states that Christ "was raised on the third day according to the Scriptures" (1 Corinthians 15:4). Paul, in this prophetic sense, may have been referring to these Old Testament Scriptures: Psalm 16:8–11, Isaiah 53:10–12, Hosea 6:2, and Jonah 1:17.

In Matthew 16:21, Jesus makes a remarkable promise. He tells his disciples that he would suffer many things at the hands of the authorities in Jerusalem and that he would even be killed. Then, he said, on the third day he would be raised to life. All the other promises Jesus made in Scripture—that our sins will be forgiven, that he is with us always, that God will provide for us—depend upon the first: his resurrection. If Christ was raised, then we can trust the Bible's promises.

Paul lays it on the line in 1 Corinthians 15:14: "If Christ has not been raised, our preaching is useless and so is your faith."

But Christ has been raised, Paul declares. Because of that fact, we can trust in the promises of the Bible.

Skeptics come and go, but the Bible survives. Respected theologian and apologist Bernard Ramm said, "A thousand times over, the death knell of the Bible has been sounded, the funeral procession formed, the inscription cut on the tombstone, and committal read. But somehow the corpse never stays put."[2]

For reflection . . .

What are your thoughts about the reliability and impact of the Bible? What effect does the resurrection of Christ have on the trustworthiness of the Bible?

chapter 8

Because of Jesus and his resurrection...

You Can Live with God's Joy

*May the God of hope fill you with all joy and
peace as you trust in him.* Romans 15:13

Martin Luther was in a rut. For days he sulked around
the house, lost in depression. Finally, one morning his wife
had enough. She came downstairs dressed in black, looking
ready for a funeral.

"Who died?" Luther asked.

"God," she replied.

Luther rebuked her, saying, "What do you mean, God
is dead? God cannot die."

"Well, the way you've been acting I was sure he had!"

I love the line I heard Brennan Manning say at a conference: "If you have the joy of the Lord in your heart, please
notify your face." Too many Christians look like poster
children for the book of Lamentations. Ask how they're
doing, and the vinegar-for-lunch bunch answers, "Pretty
good, under the circumstances."

I'm tempted to ask, "What are you doing under there?"

During some of his darkest days, the apostle Paul wrote the most positive book in the Bible: his letter to the Philippians. Repeatedly, in this brief manual on joy, Paul told the believers in Philippi to "rejoice" and to "be joyful."

Here's the remarkable thing about Philippians: Paul wrote it while in prison, literally locked in chains for preaching about Jesus. How could Paul live positively joyfully in such distressing circumstances? Because he lived firmly grounded in the power of Christ's resurrection and the assurance that Christ's resurrection guaranteed his own: "For to me, to live is Christ and to die is gain" (Philippians 1:21). In fact, for Paul, to die and be with Christ would be "better by far" (v. 23).

This life-changing letter gives us four joy builders:

God finishes what he starts. *Trust him!*
> *Being confident of this, that he who began a good work in you will carry it on to completion until the day of Christ Jesus.* Philippians 1:6

God's forgiveness is complete. *Believe him!*
> *Forgetting what is behind and straining toward what is ahead, I press on toward the goal to win the prize for which God has called me heavenward in Christ Jesus.* Philippians 3:13–14

Worry is destructive. *Release it!*
> *Do not be anxious about anything, but in every situation, by prayer and petition, with thanksgiving, present your requests to God.*
> Philippians 4:6

Gratitude is healthy. *Express it!*

> *I thank my God every time I remember you. In all*
> *my prayers for all of you, I always pray with joy*
> *because of your partnership in the gospel from the*
> *first day until now.* Philippians 1:3–5

Joy is essential to healthy living, but it's not automatic! Lack of joy ought to be a flashing warning light on the dashboard of your life. It's a sure sign you need to go back to one of the four joy builders.

For reflection . . .

How does living with God's joy affect your life? Does focusing on the truth of Christ's resurrection add joy to your life, even in unfavorable circumstances?

Which of the four joy builders do you most need to employ? How will you go about doing so?

chapter 9

Because of Jesus and his resurrection . . .

You Can Live with a Sense of Wonder

When he had led them out to the vicinity of Bethany, he lifted up his hands and blessed them. While he was blessing them, he left them and was taken up into heaven. Then they worshiped him and returned to Jerusalem with great joy. And they stayed continually at the temple, praising God. Luke 24:50–53

One of my favorite authors is Robert Fulghum, author of books such as *All I Really Need to Know I Learned in Kindergarten.*[1] (Unfortunately, I read that one after spending $30,000 on graduate school!) In his book *Uh-Oh,* Fulghum asks an interesting question: Why are five-year-olds so much more creative than college students?

Ask a kindergarten class, "How many of you can draw?" and all hands shoot up. Yes, of course we can draw—all of us. What can you draw? Anything! How about a dog eating a fire truck in a jungle? Sure! How big you want it?

How many of you can sing? All hands. Of course we sing! What can you sing? Anything! What if you don't know the words? No problem, we make them up.[2]

Fulghum goes on to say that if you ask five-year-olds if they can dance, act in a play, play a musical instrument, write poetry, read, write, or count, the answer is always the same: Yes, we can! "The children are confident in spirit, infinite in resources, and eager to learn," he says. "Everything is still possible."[3]

But ask those same questions of college kids and you'll get an entirely different answer. Almost everyone will say no. Even those who do say yes are tentative: "I can only play the piano. I can only draw horses. I can only dance to rock and roll. I sing, but only in the shower."

Then Fulghum asks a crucial question: "What went wrong between kindergarten and college? What happened to YES! of course I can?"[4]

What happened that stomped out the God-given creativity and zest for living? What happened to the enthusiasm God put into the heart of every child?

The answer is simple. We have forgotten how awesome life is. Instead, we settle for a humdrum existence, merely plodding along from day to day. We settle for routine instead of romance. We settle for low-level living instead of following our dream. We don't risk much. We don't celebrate much.

And, sadly, we don't laugh much. That may be why it's rare to find a teenager excited about becoming an adult. Who in their right mind really wants to lose their sense of wonder?

So how do we regain that sense of wonder? We remember who we are. We remember that we are God's children and that we have an incredible Father.

Walt Disney and his wife were not normal Hollywood parents. Instead of seeking the spotlight, they tried to shield their two daughters from publicity. They wanted their girls to have a normal childhood. Every day, Walt drove his kids to school. He took them to swim class and dance lessons. He arranged his schedule to take them, just as any normal father would.

In a 1956 article in *The Saturday Evening Post,* Diane Disney Miller recalled:

> Until I was six years old I didn't realize what it was that my father did for a living. The news was broken to me by a playmate at school.
>
> That night, when Dad came home from work and flopped into his easy chair, I approached him with awe. Then doubt crept in. He didn't look famous to me, he just looked tired.
>
> So I asked a critical question, "Daddy, are you Walt Disney?"
>
> "Yes, honey," he replied.
>
> "I mean, are you *the* Walt Disney?"
>
> He nodded. So it was true!
>
> "Daddy," I said, "please give me your autograph."[5]

God wants us to have a sense of wonder about who he is. Forget Walt Disney. The same God who made the universe, who raised Jesus from the dead, is our Dad. That staggering realization should fill us with awe.

The message of Easter is this: God wins. Love triumphs. Death is defeated forever.

And God, our Dad, did it.

For reflection . . .

For how much of your life have you had the creativity and confidence of a five-year-old?

What could you do to regain a childlike sense of wonder? How could reflecting on Christ's resurrection help?

chapter 10

Because of Jesus and his resurrection . . .

You Can Trust Jesus' Claims

*"Why then do you accuse me of blasphemy
because I said, 'I am God's Son'? Do not
believe me unless I do the works of my Father."*
John 10:36–37

Jesus Christ made outrageous claims. He claimed to
be able to forgive sin (Mark 2:10). He claimed to be the
way, and the truth, and the life (John 14:6). He predicted
he would be killed but then would rise from the dead
(Matthew 16:21). He even claimed to be the Son of God
(John 10:36–37).

The resurrection claim of Jesus Christ separates him
from every other religious leader. No one else—not Buddha,
Muhammad, Joseph Smith (founder of Mormonism), or
Mary Baker Eddy (founder of Christian Science)—made
such outrageous claims. No one else in history has come
back from the dead to prove his or her claims were true.

Thomas didn't believe it, however, when the other disciples told him that Jesus had risen from the dead. "Unless

I see the nail marks in his hands and put my finger where the nails were, and put my hand into his side," Thomas told them, "I will not believe" (John 20:25).

A week later, Jesus appeared and stood next to Thomas. He looked at Thomas and said, "Put your finger here; see my hands. Reach out your hand and put it into my side. Stop doubting and believe" (John 20:27).

From that moment on, Thomas was a changed man. He left that room in Jerusalem where he had seen Jesus, and he carried the message of the resurrection far and wide. According to tradition, he traveled to Babylon (now Iraq) and Persia (now Iran), and he may have traveled as far as India, telling people everywhere he went about the death and resurrection of Jesus.

What does Jesus' resurrection mean? It means that

Jesus is who he claimed to be.
> *I am the resurrection and the life. The one who believes in me will live, even though they die.* John 11:25

Jesus has the power he claimed to have.
> *All authority in heaven and on earth has been given to me.* Matthew 28:18

Jesus keeps his promises.
> *Surely I am with you always, to the very end of the age.* Matthew 28:20

What does Jesus' resurrection mean? It means you can relax—because you can trust his claims!

For reflection . . .

Have you ever struggled to accept Jesus' claims about himself? How does embracing his resurrection bridge that gap?

chapter 11

Because of Jesus and his resurrection . . .

You Can Live with God's Purpose

So I run with purpose in every step.
1 Corinthians 9:26, NLT

I love living in and being a pastor in Granite Bay, California. The town has it all: a beautiful lake, great people, wonderful weather, excellent schools. Overall, it's an idyllic American suburb. Many in our community, however, have a lot to live on and too little to live for. They have an abundance of possessions but a scarcity of purpose. And without purpose, all the possessions and possibilities are worthless.

Our culture is starving for purpose. Over the past several years, Rick Warren's book *The Purpose-Driven Life* has sold more than 25 million copies, a sure sign that millions of people are looking for meaning in life. They want something bigger to live for.

Without purpose, tragic things happen:

Life loses meaning.

> A myriad of men are born; they labor and sweat
> and struggle for bread; they squabble and scold
> and fight; they scramble for little mean advan-
> tages over each other; age creeps upon them;
> infirmities follow; . . . those they love are taken
> from them, and the joy of life is turned to aching
> grief. . . . [The release] comes at last—the only
> unpoisoned gift earth ever had for them—and
> they vanish from a world where they were of
> no consequence; where they achieved nothing;
> where they were a mistake and a failure and a
> foolishness; there they have left no sign that
> they have existed—a world which will lament
> them a day and forget them forever.[1]—Mark
> Twain (shortly before his death)

Life loses joy and significance.

> This is the true joy in life, the being used for
> a purpose recognized by yourself as a mighty
> one; the being thoroughly worn out before
> you are thrown on the scrap heap, and being
> a force of Nature instead of a feverish selfish
> little clod of ailments and grievances com-
> plaining that the world will not devote itself to
> making you happy.[2]—George Bernard Shaw

In contrast to these, focusing on Jesus and his resurrection
results in a life with passion, meaning, joy, and significance.
Living on this side of the resurrection gives us purpose.

When I was a youth pastor years ago, I took a group of teenagers from a wealthy community on a mission trip. At first, the students were disappointed. It was Sunday morning, and we had just arrived at the church in Mexico that was to serve as our headquarters for a week of ministry. The students had spent three months planning, preparing, and praying that God would use them on this trip. But something had gone wrong. The church where we were to serve had been badly burned. The roof had caved in, and only the four walls remained.

We arrived as the pastor was midway through the Sunday service. We filed into the back of the burned-out church, greeted only by the amazed stares of the nine parishioners. After a few minutes, the pastor stopped the service and asked what we were doing there.

It turned out that he had no idea we were coming. The mission board we worked with had neglected to inform him. There was a long silence, until one of the student leaders explained that we were Christians and were there to serve. I'll never forget what followed. The pastor, choking back tears, told us that some villagers had burned the church down six months earlier. "We've been praying that God would send help," he said, "but had given up hope of help ever coming!"

Our kids were stunned. Although they had heard a million times that God desired to use their lives, they were now experiencing it for the first time.

Later in a team meeting, one student said in amazement, "We are an answer to prayer!" He was right on target. Back home, these students were viewed by others, and occasionally by themselves, as problems. But when we gave them a purpose—to go out and serve in love—they became an answer to someone's prayer.

God asks something great of each of us. He made you, gave you gifts and talents, and put you right where you are—not so that you could live for yourself, but so you could be the answer to someone's prayers.

For reflection . . .

Have you ever felt that you were the answer to someone's prayers? How did that affect your inner sense of purpose?

How do you feel about the quality and intensity of your current sense of purpose and meaning in life?

Because of Jesus and his resurrection . . .

You Can Know God

Your word is a lamp for my feet, a light on my path. Psalm 119:105

"I am the light of the world." John 8:12

A little boy sat down at the kitchen table with his crayons and a big, blank sheet of paper and started to draw. His father, noticing his son hard at work, stopped to look.

"What are you doing?" he asked.

"I'm drawing a picture of God," the little boy replied.

"But, son," the father said, "you can't draw a picture of God. Nobody knows what God looks like."

The little boy thought for a moment, and then said, "Well, they will when I get through!"

There are a lot of false, sometimes bizarre, ideas about God circulating in the world. Most of them sound as if they were made up, out of thin air, much like the picture drawn by the little boy.

Times haven't changed. Back in 1947, C. S. Lewis told *Time* magazine that he knew of a girl whose "higher thinking" parents brought her up to regard God as perfect "substance." The problem, the girl told Lewis, was that she ended up thinking of God as something like a vast tapioca pudding. To make matters worse, Lewis said, she disliked tapioca![1]

Some think of God as an angry judge who sits on his throne, just waiting for us to do something wrong so he can zap us from on high. No wonder people run from God, fear God, and avoid church like the plague.

With all these misconceptions of what God is like, "This is the day the Lord has made" has turned into "This is the Lord that the day has made." The problem with all this is that it's possible to be sincere yet sincerely wrong. We need an authoritative word from one with the credibility of rising from the dead.

Jesus showed us a very different view of God. He shattered the myths built about God. While many believe that God is distant and detached, the Bible calls Jesus "Emmanuel," which means "God with us" (Matthew 1:23). Instead of an uncaring cosmic force, Jesus showed us a God who knows every detail of our lives. "Even the very hairs of your head are all numbered," Jesus told his followers (Matthew 10:30).

Having a clear view of God puts the world in proper perspective, even as turning on the light in a dark room helps us see things as they really are.

My daughter Leslie knows how important a clear view can be. One night her kids were complaining about mosquitoes in their room. Rather than turning on the light and risk having the kids wide awake for the rest of the night, she decided to go into their room and spray insect repellent in the dark. When she finished, she went to bed.

The next morning Leslie discovered, to her horror, that she had covered the bedding, the bedroom walls, and the kids with blue spray paint. "I thought it smelled kind of funny," she said later.

Life doesn't work well when you can't see clearly! If you don't know Jesus Christ, you're in the dark. You're just kind of stumbling along through life, unable to see God or understand your purpose in life. You can't see clearly until you know "the light of the world."

Do you want to get to know God? It's simple. Get to know Jesus Christ. Jesus said, "Anyone who has seen me has seen the Father" (John 14:9).

For reflection . . .

How does Christ's resurrection intensify the reality that he is "God with us"?

What misconceptions of God have you struggled with? Have those struggles been resolved? What do you need to build into your life that would help you get to know God better?

chapter 13

Because of Jesus and his resurrection . . .

You Can Live with God's Guidance and Direction

Do not conform to the pattern of this world, but be transformed by the renewing of your mind. Then you will be able to test and approve what God's will is—his good, pleasing and perfect will. Romans 12:2

I remember hearing an enlightening poem penned by the eminent theologian, Dr. Seuss. In that story, a creature called a Zode comes to a fork in the road and can't make up his mind which way to go. So in the end he decides to try to take both roads at the same time. Dr. Seuss concludes the poem in his inimitable style with embarrassing misfortune befalling the waffling Zode.

Many of us are like that Zode: getting nowhere spiritually because we can't make a decision. We're like the man who went to see a psychiatrist for advice because he was having trouble making up his mind.

"Are you indecisive?" the psychiatrist asked him.

"Yes and no," the man replied.

"What do you mean by that?" the doctor inquired.

"Well, I used to be indecisive. But now I'm not sure."

Talk about paralysis by analysis!

These days, people try all kinds of systems, looking for guidance: astrology, numerology, metaphysics, even psychic hotlines. As we pursue God's best for our lives, the following three principles can help cut through the fog:

God's will is found in God's Word, the Bible.

As we read his Word, God speaks to us. If we ignore God's Word, we ignore God. Through the principles, commands, and examples of Scripture, we discover God's will.

God's will never contradicts God's Word.

People often tell me they "feel" God leading them in a certain direction. My first reaction is always the same: "What does the Bible say about it?" We can save a lot of confusion by asking that one simple question. If we dedicate and conform our minds to God's Word, we will know God's will.

God's will is revealed to us by the Holy Spirit.

> One of the wonderful benefits of Christ's resurrection is that it resulted in God sending us the Holy Spirit. Just before Jesus was crucified, he promised his disciples that the Father would give them an advocate, or counselor, to help them and to be with them forever (John 14:16). And Jesus said that "when he, the Spirit of truth, comes, he will guide you into all the truth" (John 16:13). We're not left on our own to figure out God's will. The risen Christ has sent us the Spirit of truth to help us and guide us!

Granted, we can't find a spot in the Bible to answer every specific question we may face. Perhaps you're facing some questions such as these: Do I look for another job? What school should we send our children to? Do we invest in an IRA, or do we replace the windows of our house?

When facing such questions, ask yourself if there are any principles, commands, or examples of Scripture that apply. Trust the Holy Spirit to guide you. Be open to the ways God leads us through the wisdom of fellow believers.

Our destinies are determined not by chance, but by the choices we make. Choose wisely. Find God's will for your life in God's Word, applied to specific situations through God's Spirit.

For reflection . . .

Have you ever looked for guidance in the wrong kind of
system? Are you making wise choices in that regard now?

Are you adequately interacting with God's Word and
God's Spirit in order to determine God's will for your life?

chapter 14

Because of Jesus and his resurrection . . .

You Can Live with Passion

Never be lacking in zeal, but keep your spiritual fervor, serving the Lord. Romans 12:11

Many years ago, an anonymous exhausted person wrote the following:

> Yes, I'm tired. For several years I've been blaming it on middle age, iron-poor blood, lack of vitamins, air pollution, water pollution, saccharin, obesity, dieting, underarm odor, yellow wax build-up, and a dozen other maladies that make you wonder if life is really worth living.
>
> But now I find out that I'm tired because I'm overworked.
>
> The population of this country is 200 million. Eighty-four million are retired. That leaves 116 million to do the work. There are 75 million in school, which leaves 41 million

to do the work. Of this total, there are 22 million employed by the federal government.

That leaves 19 million to do the work. Four million are in the armed forces, which leaves 15 million to do the work. Take from that total the 14,800,000 people who work for the state and city governments and that leaves 200,000 to do the work. There are 188,000 in hospitals, so that leaves 12,000 to do the work. Now, there are 11,998 people in prisons.

That leaves just two people to do the work. You and me. And you're sitting there reading this. No wonder I'm tired.

Many of us can relate. We're worn out. We're living at a hamster's pace, racing faster and faster yet getting nowhere—and losing our passion for God and life in the process.

Paul warned about this condition when he exhorted the believers in Rome: "Never be lacking in zeal, but keep your spiritual fervor" (Romans 12:11). The key word is *keep*. That means it's not automatic—you don't stay on fire for God automatically. You can lose your enthusiasm for God and start going through the motions.

The disciples felt that way. When Jesus died, they lost their zeal for living and faced a future without hope or purpose. When Jesus rose from the grave, the disciples were reborn. They were ready to live out Jesus' commandments: "Love the Lord your God with all your heart and with all your soul and with all your mind and with all your strength" and "Love your neighbor as yourself" (Mark 12:30–31). Feel the passion in those statements?

A survey of the New Testament reveals that God does not want us to live life in a halfhearted way. God knows that passion is essential for both personal transformation and social impact. Following the resurrection, the early church exploded in resurrection power (detailed in the book of Acts). What was the early church's secret? Passion.

While reading the book of Acts, ask yourself, "What did these first believers *not have?*" They had no financial backing, attractive buildings, organizational structure, denominational support, seminary training, church boards, microphones, video capability, or IT department. They lacked a stable economy, favorable governmental conditions, and supportive media.

And yet, against all odds, in a relatively short account, the early church exploded to thirty-two countries, fifty-four cities, and nine islands—all the way to Rome, the capital of the world at that time. What the early believers *did have* was an impact, and they had an impact because they had passion. G. K. Chesterton once said, "Jesus promised his disciples three things—that they would be completely fearless, absurdly happy, and in constant trouble."

I believe the number one need in the church today is to recapture the kind of passion the early believers had. And, the number one need in most communities is a church whose members are passionate about bringing the love of Christ to their community.

I just returned from Rome, Paris, London, Zurich, Munich, and Florence, where I saw cathedral after cathedral, complete with magnificent architecture and art, stunning stained glass windows, beautiful icons, religious pageantry and rituals, and historical significance. As magnificent as those buildings are, however, many of them are void of people. These cathedrals have everything—except the hearts and minds of people in the community. Why? Somewhere along the way, the church lost its passion.

Here's why this is so important. When Christians in churches avoid growing lukewarm and instead are filled with passion, communities are touched and transformed, marriages are helped and healed, and people far from God have their lives and eternal destinations changed. The poor are lifted, children are loved, teenagers are developed, people's gifts are deployed, and folks discover the thrill of returning to the state of the early church—where communities were changed by the resurrection power of Jesus Christ, working through God's people who were filled with passion. *That's why the number one need in America right now is for God's people to catch fire once again.*

God wants us to have wholehearted passion, the kind of passion that can make a difference in both our own lives and in the world.

For reflection . . .

What are people in our society passionate about?

Would you say that you have a spiritual zeal and passion for God, or are you just going through the motions? What can you do to reenergize and renew your spiritual passion?

chapter 15

Because of Jesus and his resurrection . . .

You Can Overcome Discouragement

*The LORD himself goes before you and will be
with you; he will never leave you nor forsake
you. Do not be afraid; do not be discouraged.*
Deuteronomy 31:8

As the father of four, I love the following story.

Four expectant fathers sat in a hospital waiting room while their wives were in labor. The
nurse arrived and announced to the first man,
"Congratulations, sir! You're the father of
twins."

"What a coincidence!" the man said. "I
work for the Minnesota Twins baseball team."

A little while later the nurse returned with
news for the second man: "You, sir, are the
father of triplets."

"Wow! That's an incredible coincidence,"
he responded. "I work for 3M."

An hour later the nurse came back. This time she turned to the third man, who had been waiting quietly in the corner. His wife, she said, had just given birth to quadruplets. He responded with stunned silence.

"Don't tell me—another coincidence?" the nurse asked.

"I don't believe it," he said, after regaining his composure. "I work for the Four Seasons Hotel."

At this, the fourth man let out a scream and fainted dead away. The nurse rushed to his side. When he regained consciousness, he mumbled over and over, "Why did I take that job at 7-Eleven?"

Ever felt like that man? Life can suddenly get overwhelming. Hope can quickly turn to discouragement.

Rick Warren describes discouragement as a "disease" unique to human beings. Although curable, discouragement is universal, contagious, and deadly. We all catch this disease—and we can come down with it more than once. It's highly contagious; think about how easy it is to get discouraged when you're around someone who is discouraged. And discouragement is deadly; it can wreck your life and ruin your relationships.[1]

As a pastor, I've seen more people walk away from God, marriage, and effective living because of discouragement than for any other factor. That's why we, at Bayside Church, constantly give people the following definition of discouragement:

"Discouragement is the anesthetic the devil uses on a person just before he reaches in and carves out their heart."

The root problem with discouragement is this: People give up! They give up on God. On their marriage. On their kids. On their church. On their ministry. Even on life itself.

Discouraged? Maybe the following parable will help.

> One day a farmer's mule fell into a well. The farmer heard the mule braying (or whatever mules do when they fall into wells). After assessing the situation, the farmer sympathized with the mule but decided that neither the mule nor the well was worth the trouble of saving. So, he called his neighbors together, told them what had happened, and enlisted their help to haul dirt to bury the old mule in the well and put him out of his misery.
>
> Initially, the old mule brayed hysterically. But as the farmer and his neighbors continued shoveling, and as the dirt hit the mule's back, a thought struck him: *Every time a shovel load of dirt lands on my back, I will shake it off and step up!* This he did, blow after blow.
>
> "Shake it off and step up! Shake it off and step up!" the mule repeated to encourage himself. No matter how painful the blows or how distressing the situation, the old mule fought panic and kept right on shaking it off and stepping up. It wasn't long before the old mule, battered and exhausted, stepped triumphantly over the wall of that well.

What seemed that it would bury the mule actually blessed him . . . all because of the manner in which the old mule handled his adversity. That's life! *If we refuse to give in to discouragement and self-pity, the adversities that come along to bury us usually have, within them, the potential to benefit and bless us!*

Now, back up two thousand years. It's the first Easter, and everything has gone wrong. On Palm Sunday, Jesus is practically crowned king. Five days later, he's dead, and the disciples are hunted criminals.

On Easter Sunday, when the disciples saw Jesus alive, their hope and confidence were restored. Two of the disciples described their encounter with Jesus this way: "Were not our hearts burning within us while he talked with us on the road and opened the Scriptures to us?" (Luke 24:32).

God wants to set our hearts on fire, so we can serve him with confidence and joy.

The prophet Isaiah told us that God "gives strength to the weary and increases the power of the weak. Even youths grow tired and weary, and young men stumble and fall; but those who hope in the LORD will renew their strength. They will soar on wings like eagles; they will run and not grow weary, they will walk and not be faint" (Isaiah 40:29–31).

For reflection . . .

Recall a discouraging time in your life. How did you overcome the discouragement?

In what way are you facing discouragement now? How could focusing on the resurrection of Jesus help you?

chapter 16

Because of Jesus and his resurrection . . .

You Can Overcome Fear

I sought the LORD, and he answered me; he delivered me from all my fears. Psalm 34:4

It's embarrassing to admit, but I'm a recovering coward. Sixteen years ago I was having a great time *not* being a pastor. I was speaking, writing, and, in general, having a blast. Then, my wife, Carol, and I were invited to start a church in Granite Bay, California. I immediately applied this verse: "'Lord, here am I'—send someone else!" And I turned down the invitation.

Truth be told, I was afraid. Afraid of failing. Afraid no one would show up. Afraid of raising money. Afraid that because the new church was in California, we would be sued in the process. (That happened, by the way.)

Plus, I was a dad with four young kids. Dads with four young kids don't start churches. It's far too risky.

I then made the mistake of attending a three-day prayer summit with eight hundred Christian leaders from around the world. Three hours into a late-night prayer meeting I had prayed for everything I could think of—twice! Then this idea occurred to me: *I should pray for Bayside, the new church, that God would give them the right pastor,* because it sure wasn't going to be me!

While I was praying, I heard God speak to me. The message was clear: *Read Acts 18.* I opened my Bible and read the following: "Do not be afraid; keep on speaking; do not be silent. For I am with you, and no one is going to attack and harm you, because I have many people in this city" (Acts 18:9–10). I believe God said to me, *If you accept this invitation to plant a church, I will rally people to help you.*

But I still didn't want to plant the church. So, I decided to keep reading, looking for a loophole. I didn't find one. Instead, the next verse said, "So Paul stayed for a year and a half, teaching them the word of God" (Acts 18:11).

I walked out of that prayer meeting and called my wife to find out if I had really heard from God. (You husbands will understand.) Carol said she had felt God calling us to start the church and wondered when I would figure it out.

The rest is history. Bayside is the best thing that has happened in all my years of ministry. The church exploded out of the gate. Thousands of people have come to Christ, including some relatives for whom we had been praying for more than twenty years. These have been the best sixteen years of my life, but I almost missed them for one reason: *fear.*

The problem with fear is this: Fear paralyzes. Fear is a self-imposed prison where confidence and hope are locked out, and fear and anxiety are locked in. Fear will keep you from discovering God's vision for your life and from experiencing the best years of your life.

Remember these truths:

The first words the angel spoke to the women after Jesus Christ rose from the dead were "Do not be afraid." Matthew 28:1-7

The first words Jesus spoke to his disciples after he rose from the grave were "Peace be with you!" Luke 24:36

At Bayside, we also have a definition for fear: "Fear is the darkroom where negativity develops."

Is God calling you to start something, to serve somewhere, or to give something—but you're afraid to launch? If so, go for it! You could be on the first day of the best sixteen-year run of your life!

Jesus Christ is risen from the dead. Do not be afraid.

For reflection . . .

When have you experienced the paralyzing grip of fear?

What would it look like in your life if, today, you heard Jesus say to you, "Don't be afraid"?

chapter 17

Because of Jesus and his resurrection . . .

You Can Trust God's Promises

Jesus performed many other signs in the presence
of his disciples, which are not recorded in this
book. But these are written that you may believe
that Jesus is the Messiah, the Son of God, and
that by believing you may have life in his name.
John 20:30–31

In his book *When All You've Ever Wanted Isn't Enough,*
Rabbi Harold S. Kushner tells the following story:

I was sitting on a beach one summer day,
watching two children, a boy and a girl,
playing in the sand. They were hard at work
building an elaborate sand castle by the water's
edge, with gates and towers and moats and
internal passages. Just when they had nearly
finished their project, a big wave came along
and knocked it down, reducing it to a heap of
wet sand. I expected the children to burst into
tears, devastated by what had happened to all

their hard work. But they surprised me. Instead, they ran up the shore away from the water, laughing and holding hands, and sat down to build another castle. I realized that they had taught me an important lesson. All the things in our lives, all the complicated structures we spent so much time and energy creating, are built on sand. Only our relationships to other people endure. Sooner or later, the wave will come along and knock down what we have worked so hard to build up. When that happens, only the person who has somebody's hand to hold will be able to laugh.[1]

During the storms of life, we need something firm to hold on to. Nothing lifts my spirit more than holding on to God's promises. God has promises for almost every circumstance. Let me give you some examples:

Every time you pick up a Bible, remember Jesus' promise in Matthew 24:35:

"Heaven and earth will pass away, but my words will never pass away."

Every time you come to worship, remember Jesus' promise in Matthew 18:20:

"Where two or three gather in my name, there am I with them."

Every time you feel alone, remember Jesus' promise in Matthew 28:20:

> "Surely I am with you always, to the very end of the age."

Every time you feel weak, remember God's promise in 2 Thessalonians 3:3:

> "The Lord is faithful, and he will strengthen you and protect you from the evil one."

Every time you have failed, remember God's promise in 1 John 1:9:

> "If we confess our sins, he is faithful and just and will forgive us our sins and purify us from all unrighteousness."

Every time you are tempted to lose hope, remember God's promise in Hebrews 10:23:

> "Let us hold unswervingly to the hope we profess, for he who promised is faithful."

And when you stand on the brink of death, remember Paul's promise in Philippians 3:20-21:

> The Lord Jesus Christ . . . by the power that enables him to bring everything under his control, will transform our lowly bodies so that they will be like his glorious body.

One Scripture sums it up: "The LORD's lovingkindnesses indeed never cease, for His compassions never fail. They are new every morning; great is Your faithfulness" (Lamentations 3:22–23, NASB).

For reflection . . .

How does Christ's resurrection infuse God's promises with power and vitality?

Read again the biblical promises listed above. Which promise is most relevant and valuable to you today? What difference would trust in that promise make in your life?

chapter 18

Because of Jesus and his resurrection . . .

You Can Change Direction

*". . . neither do I condemn you," Jesus declared.
"Go now and leave your life of sin."* John 8:11

*Therefore, if anyone is in Christ, the new
creation has come: The old has gone, the new is
here!* 2 Corinthians 5:17

The most discouraging words in the English language
are these: "You will never change!" Those four words destroy lives. They steal vitality. They replace clear hope for
a better future with the icy fog of confusion and despair.

Jesus never uttered those words! Whenever he came
across someone who had failed or who had lost hope, he
offered that person the chance to start again.

In John 8, the Jewish religious leaders brought before
Jesus a woman who had been caught in bed with a man
who wasn't her husband. (Note that the man with whom
she was involved was nowhere to be found.) Surely the
entire "affair" was staged: the religious leaders were trying

to trap Jesus. If he ruled to stone the woman, he would be challenging the Roman authorities, who didn't permit Jews to carry out death sentences. But if Jesus said she should not be stoned, he could be charged with disregarding the Law of Moses.

Jesus said, "Fine, go ahead. There's just one catch. Let any one of you who is without sin be the first to throw a stone at her."

Once the crowd dispersed—leaving behind a large pile of unused stones—Jesus looked at the woman and said, "Woman, where are they? Has no one condemned you?"

"No one, sir," she answered.

"Then neither do I condemn you," Jesus told her. "Go now and leave your life of sin."

Not only did Jesus show mercy to this woman, but he also invited her to change direction and start again.

Earl Palmer tells one of my favorite stories. He and several friends from the West Coast attended seminary on the East Coast. Holidays meant an occasion to pile in a car and head home. Wanting to get there as fast as possible, they drove straight through, each taking a three-hour turn behind the wheel while the other guys slept.

During one of their trips home, Earl was driving through Iowa in the middle of the night when he passed a gas station. The car was low on gas, and it was about time to change drivers, so Earl made a U-turn. He went back to the gas station and filled up the tank, then woke the next driver, climbed into the backseat, and fell fast asleep.

Since Earl neglected to mention the U-turn, his friend spent three hours driving east as fast as he could, with no idea he was heading in the wrong direction. About six in the morning, the friend began to suspect he was heading the wrong way. He woke Earl only to discover that his worst fears were realized. Earl's friend sheepishly admitted he had ignored several signs indicating he was headed in the wrong direction: mileage signs, road signs, even a Greyhound bus going by with "Las Vegas" on the destination sign.

"I ignored all those signs until I saw the sunrise in my windshield," he said. "When I saw the sun come up, that was too big a sign to ignore."

The Son of God rising from the grave at Easter is too big a sign to ignore. It should capture our attention and cause us to pull over and rethink the direction of our lives.

The good news is that God allows U-turns, no matter how long we've been driving in the wrong direction.

For reflection . . .

How was Jesus able to challenge and confront sin without making a person feel condemned?

What is the most drastic U-turn your life direction has taken? Does the current direction of your life need to change in any way?

Because of Jesus and his resurrection . . .

You Can Experience God's Presence

"And surely I am with you always, to the very end of the age." Matthew 28:20

Newlywed Nora Nagaruk's plans and dreams were coming true. Ever since she was a teenager growing up in a small village in Alaska, Nora had dreamed of becoming a doctor. By the summer of 2004, she had completed eleven years of training: four years at the University of Oklahoma, another four at the University of Washington School of Medicine, a year of internship, and two years of residency. One more year of residency, and her lifelong goal of being a doctor would become a reality.

Then, just before her first wedding anniversary, Nora came down with what she thought was a bad cold. When it didn't go away, she went in for a few tests, convinced that her nagging sore throat and fatigue indicated a case of mononucleosis or perhaps strep throat. Due to the demands of her residency, Nora often slept only a couple of hours at night. She thought the lack of sleep had finally caught up to her.

Tests for mono and strep throat came back negative. Meanwhile, Nora's sickness worsened. "It was as if the life was being taken out of me," she said. Finally, a blood test revealed acute myelocytic leukemia—the same cancer that had killed her father twenty-five years earlier and her nephew four years earlier. A few days later, she was on a flight from Alaska to Seattle to begin cancer treatments.

Faced with this life-threatening illness, Nora and her husband, Nathan, could have been overwhelmed. But from the first days in the hospital, their friends and family surrounded them with love and support. They visited, called, e-mailed, and, most importantly, prayed for Nora.

The illness changed the way Nora viewed God. At the worst moment, when all her dreams were snatched away and death seemed just a step away, God was with her.

"You know things about God's character—that he is loving and caring," she said, "but when you are lying in a hospital bed and you can feel people praying for you, it's like God has come down to my bedside."[1]

By the way, Nora's cancer went into remission, she realized her dream of becoming a doctor, and she now practices family medicine in Anchorage!

On the first Easter, the followers of Jesus made some amazing discoveries; but none was greater than this: *the presence of Jesus is real.* Just as Nora discovered God when at her lowest moment, so the disciples also found Jesus when all their hopes were dashed.

Are you locked in a room and filled with fear? Jesus is there. Weeping in a graveyard? Jesus is there. Filled with doubt? Jesus is there. Lying in a hospital bed? Jesus is there.

No matter what your circumstances, Jesus' promise holds true: "Surely I am with you always, to the very end of the age" (Matthew 28:20).

For reflection . . .

When have you sensed the presence of the risen Christ in the midst of a crisis or low time?

chapter 20

Because of Jesus and his resurrection . . .

You Can Stop Worrying

> *Do not be anxious about anything, but in every situation, by prayer and petition, with thanksgiving, present your requests to God.*
> Philippians 4:6

> *Someone has said that the average person is crucifying himself between two thieves: the regrets of yesterday and the worries about tomorrow.*[1] Warren Wiersbe

Several years ago I preached a sermon entitled "Why Pray When You Can Worry?" The point was this: worry is life's most useless activity. There are three huge problems with choosing anxiety as a lifestyle.

Worry doesn't work.

> Jesus put it this way: "Can any one of you by worrying add a single hour to your life?" (Matthew 6:27). Worrying cannot make me taller or smarter or lengthen my life. One

person described worry like this: "Worry is like a rocking chair; it will give me something to do, but it won't get me anywhere." Worry can not change the past. Worry can not control the future. The only thing worry can change is *me*—it makes me miserable in the present.

Worry is destructive.

Anxiety saps us of the emotional energy it takes to tackle the problems we worry about. It's like the hypochondriac who put on his tombstone, "I told you I was sick." Concentration camp survivor Corrie ten Boom wisely spoke of worry: "Worry does not empty tomorrow of its sorrows; it empties today of its strength."

Worry dishonors God.

Jesus was even more forceful: "Why do you worry about clothes?" he asked. "See how the flowers of the field grow. They do not labor or spin. Yet I tell you that not even Solomon in all his splendor was dressed like one of these. If that is how God clothes the grass of the field, which is here today and tomorrow is thrown into the fire, will he not much more clothe you—you of little faith?" (Matthew 6:28–30). Worry dishonors God because worry is practical atheism.

Christ's resurrection demonstrates that even in the darkest of circumstances, God can still work. As George Müller said,

"The beginning of anxiety is the end of faith, and the beginning of true faith is the end of anxiety."

Granted, for many of us, exercising courageous faith is easier said than done. We may need to take baby steps as we move from worry to faith. Simply setting aside time for solitude and prayer is a clear step in the right direction. Nevertheless, wonderful assurance comes to us because of Christ's resurrection. (See the previous chapter, "You Can Experience God's Presence," and Jesus' promise to his disciples: "I am with you always.")

We will struggle with anxiety less as we trust God more.

For reflection . . .

Some have labeled our era the age of anxiety. What factors do you think cause such high levels of anxiety? What impact should a relationship with Christ have in this area?

What does "worry is practical atheism" mean? What steps can you take to move away from that kind of unbelief?

chapter 21

Because of Jesus and his resurrection . . .

You Can Let Go of Guilt

*Therefore, there is now no condemnation for
those who are in Christ Jesus.* Romans 8:1

Two young brothers, ages eight and ten, could
not stay out of trouble. Any mischief going
on in their neighborhood, everyone knew
these boys were behind it. Exasperated, their
mother asked a local pastor who had a reputa-
tion for getting children to behave if he would
speak with her boys. He agreed, but asked to
see them individually.

The next morning, the mother sent in her
eight-year-old, with the older boy scheduled
to see the pastor in the afternoon. The pastor,
a huge man with a booming voice, sat the
younger boy down and asked him sternly,
"Where is God?"

The boy's mouth dropped, but he made no response. He just sat with his mouth hanging open and his eyes bugging out.

The pastor repeated the question in a more stern tone. "Where is God?" he demanded.

Again, no answer.

Frustrated, the pastor shook his finger in the boy's face and bellowed, "Where is God?"

The boy screamed as he bolted from the room, ran home, dove into his closet, and slammed the door behind him. When his older brother found him, he asked, "What happened?"

The younger brother, gasping for breath, replied: "We are in big trouble this time. God is missing—and they think we did it!"

Peter could relate. He was in trouble, and he knew it.

Jesus had told his disciples that he would be arrested and that they would all abandon him. Peter in reply had pledged to Jesus his allegiance; but instead, Peter denied Jesus three times. Worst of all, after Peter's third denial, Jesus looked right at him (Luke 22:61).

Overcome, Peter did what most of us would do. He ran away.

Guilt can have that effect on us. By keeping us focused on past failures, guilt prevents us from moving forward. Guilt traps us in an endless cycle of failure, regret, and embarrassment.

The million-dollar question is this: How can we break free from guilt?

We know from Luke 24:34 and 1 Corinthians 15:5 that the risen Christ made a special appearance just to Peter on Easter Sunday. Though the Scriptures give us no details of this encounter, surely Peter's guilt was addressed. Regardless, notice how Jesus, some time later, therapeutically freed Peter from guilt. When Peter and six of his fellow disciples were fishing on the Sea of Galilee, Jesus provided a miraculous catch of fish for them and served them breakfast. Jesus then initiated the following conversation:

> *When they had finished eating, Jesus said to Simon Peter, "Simon son of John, do you truly love me more than these?"*
>
> *"Yes, Lord," he said, "you know that I love you."*
>
> *Jesus said, "Feed my lambs."*
>
> *Again Jesus said, "Simon son of John, do you love me?"*
>
> *He answered, "Yes, Lord, you know that I love you."*
>
> *Jesus said, "Take care of my sheep."*
>
> *The third time he said to him, "Simon son of John, do you love me?"*
>
> *Peter was hurt because Jesus asked him the third time, "Do you love me?" He said, "Lord, you know all things; you know that I love you."*
>
> *Jesus said, "Feed my sheep."* John 21:15–17

Amazing! Jesus asked Peter three present-tense questions and then gave him three future-tense assignments. Not one word about his past! Not one word about his failure! *Jesus resolved and forgave Peter's past, moved him into the present, and pointed him to the future.* That is God's key to escaping the prison of guilt!

Later, perhaps the apostle Paul was thinking of his own sinful past, particularly his zeal to destroy Christians, when he penned this great guilt-destroying, life-giving prescription: "Forgetting what is behind and straining toward what is ahead, I press on toward the goal to win the prize for which God has called me heavenward in Christ Jesus" (Philippians 3:13–14).

For reflection . . .

Why is guilt such a destructive emotion?

How does pressing toward the prize of our own resurrection help destroy guilt and give us life?

chapter 22

Because of Jesus and his resurrection . . .

You Can Experience Real Peace

*On the evening of that first day of the week,
when the disciples were together, with the doors
locked for fear of the Jewish leaders, Jesus came
and stood among them and said, "Peace be
with you!" After he said this, he showed them
his hands and side. The disciples were overjoyed
when they saw the Lord.*

*Again Jesus said, "Peace be with you! As the
Father has sent me, I am sending you."* John
20:19–21

*Let the peace of Christ rule in your hearts,
since as members of one body you were called to
peace. And be thankful.* Colossians 3:15

Mary Taylor Previte, great-granddaughter of J. Hudson
Taylor, grew up in China with her missionary parents.
During World War II, Mary, at age nine, was taken captive
and put in a Japanese POW camp, the Weihsien internment

camp in present-day Weifang, China. She spent three years in the camp and was separated from her parents for even longer. Mary didn't see her father for over five years.

That kind of trauma could haunt a child for years and leave that child constantly fearful, unable to find real peace. But in her book, *Hungry Ghosts,* Mary said she found strength and peace in the prison camp.

> Awash in a cesspool of every kind of misery, Weihsien was daily triumphs—earthy victories over bedbugs and rats and flies. If you had bedbugs, you launched the Battle of the Bedbugs each Saturday. With knife or thumbnail you attacked each seam of your blanket or pillow, killing the bugs and eggs in your path. . . .
>
> I entrusted my anxieties to our teachers in the belief that they would take care of us. Our teachers could fix everything. Or if they couldn't, *God* would.
>
> Our spirits could scamper to the heavens atop the hundreds and hundreds of God's promises like *All things work together for good to them that love God.* We could tell endless chains of Bible stories of God's rescuing His people: Moses leading God's children out of slavery into their Promised Land. The ravens feeding the hungry prophet Elijah in the wilderness. God's closing the mouths of the lions to protect Daniel in the lions' den. We could move mountains.

> You could breathe the anticipation: God was
> going to add our very own story to the miracles
> of the ages.[1]

Years later, Mary became the director of New Jersey's
Camden County Youth Center, where children arrested for
violent crimes are held before standing trial. A hopeless,
violent facility when she arrived, the center was transformed
into a place where broken children could be restored. Having
experienced God's peace in a POW camp in China, Mary
brought that peace into the lives of children in a New Jersey
juvenile detention center.

The world offers us another kind of peace. Some people
look for peace by drinking enough to become numb. Others
search for peace in one relationship after another, hoping
someone will fill the void in their lives. Some people try to
find peace in busyness or possessions, but they come up empty
every time.

Only in the resurrection of Jesus Christ will we find last-
ing, authentic peace.

Real peace is found in knowing Jesus Christ, God's Son.

Real peace means knowing that no matter what we do,
God will not stop loving us.

Real peace is hearing the risen Christ say, "Peace be with
you!" (John 20:19), when we are afraid.

Real peace is knowing that no matter what happens in
the future, God will give us strength to handle it.

Real peace means that our lives and our families are safe in God's hands.

The apostle Paul told us of God's peace in Philippians 4:5–7: "The Lord is near. Do not be anxious about anything, but in every situation, by prayer and petition, with thanksgiving, present your requests to God. And the peace of God, which transcends all understanding, will guard your hearts and your minds in Christ Jesus."

That's real peace!

For reflection . . .

What difference have you experienced between the peace that the world offers and the peace that Jesus offers?

chapter 23

Because of Jesus and his resurrection . . .

You Can Expect Great Things from God

"Nothing is impossible with God."
Luke 1:37, NLT

One day in 1939, doctoral student George Bernard Dantzig arrived late for Professor Jerzy Neyman's graduate-level statistics class at the University of California, Berkeley. On the blackboard were two mathematical problems, which Dantzig assumed to be homework assignments. He wrote them down in his notebook and spent the next few days trying to solve them.

"A few days later," Dantzig told the *College Mathematics Journal*, "I apologized to Neyman for taking so long to do the homework—the problems seemed to be a little harder than usual. I asked him if he still wanted it. He told me to throw it on his desk. I did so reluctantly because his desk was covered with such a heap of papers that I feared my homework would be lost there forever."

Six weeks later, Dantzig was awakened one Sunday morning by someone pounding on his front door. It was Professor Neyman. "He rushed in with papers in hand, all excited," Dantzig recalled. It turned out that Dantzig had made a mistake. The problems on the blackboard hadn't been homework assignments at all. They were two famed "unsolvable problems"—that had baffled mathematicians for years.

Years later, Dantzig admitted that if he'd known the problems were "unsolvable," he probably would have grown discouraged and given up on solving them. Instead, because he expected to solve them, he worked at them until he did.[1]

The Bible is filled with accounts of people who defied expectations. No one thought that David stood a chance against Goliath. No one gave Moses half a chance of setting his people free. No one expected Jesus to walk out of the grave on Easter Sunday. But David slew Goliath, Moses freed the Israelites, and *Jesus rose from the grave, proving that nothing is impossible—with God.*

No one expected much of William Carey, either. Born in 1761, he spent most of his early career as a shoemaker in England. He had limited formal education, little money, and no influence. But one day he starting thinking about Jesus' command to go into the whole world and preach the good news. *Surely,* he thought to himself, *Jesus meant what he said.*

At a meeting of church leaders, Carey, a newly ordained minister, stood to argue for the value of overseas missions. He was interrupted by an older minister who said, "Young man, sit down! When God wants to convert the heathen, he will do it without consulting you or me."

At this time in history, churches were not sending missionaries. Nevertheless, Carey refused to give up. He kept praying, and he never gave up on his dream. "Expect great things from God; attempt great things for God!" became his motto.

Finally, in 1793 he set sail for India, where he eventually founded a school, became an expert on the local Bengali language, and led many people to Christ. He translated the Bible into Bengali and started a movement to end the practice of "sati," or widow burnings. Tens of thousands of missionaries would follow his example—and the message of Jesus spread around the world.

Expect great things from God. Attempt great things for God. Because Christ's resurrection reminds us that nothing is impossible with God.

For reflection . . .

Why do so few Christians dream big?

What "great things" do you believe God might have in store for your future?

chapter 24

Because of Jesus and his resurrection . . .

You Can Experience Hope

*"For I know the plans I have for you," declares
the Lord, "plans to prosper you and not to
harm you, plans to give you hope and a future."*
Jeremiah 29:11

Joseph had high hopes. Handsome and smart, he was
his father's favorite son. He also had dreams that eventually
came true. Twice he dreamed that all eleven of his brothers
would bow before him, a dream that didn't go over well
with his brothers. So, they sold him into slavery (a solution
many parents of teenagers have contemplated!).

Being sold into slavery in Egypt was only the beginning of Joseph's troubles. When he refused to have an affair
with his master's wife, she falsely accused him of trying to
assault her. Joseph was tossed in jail. He remained there for
years, with no hope of ever getting out.

But then his big break came. Pharaoh was haunted by
nightmares and needed someone to interpret them, but
no one could. Finally, Pharaoh's cupbearer—the guy who

ensured the king's drinks weren't poisoned—who had been in jail with Joseph until two years earlier, mentioned Joseph to his boss. The cupbearer knew firsthand about Joseph's knack for interpreting dreams. Soon Joseph was brought before Pharaoh. When he correctly interpreted Pharaoh's dreams, telling him that seven years of famine were on the way, Pharaoh responded by making Joseph his right-hand man and putting him in charge of famine preparations.

The famine did come. And sure enough, when Joseph's brothers needed food, they traveled to Egypt to buy grain. There, not recognizing Joseph, they bowed before their brother.

Through all his years of suffering, Joseph's hope never failed. As one gospel song puts it, in the midnight hour God turned things around.

Time and again in the Bible, *God did great things through people who suffered but never lost hope.* And many times God acted when circumstances seemed darkest:

- Before Abraham became the father of many nations —*he and Sarah were childless.*
- Before Moses led Israel out of Egypt—*he was a fugitive running for his life.*
- Before Hosea became a powerful spokesman for God—*his adulterous wife betrayed him.*
- Before Peter preached before thousands—*he denied his Savior three times.*

All of these people found hope in their darkest hour. *Hope* is a powerful word. Hope helps us keep going through our toughest battles. Hope helps us climb over obstacles when others have given up. Jim Wallis defines hope this way: believing, in spite of the evidence, and then watching the evidence change.

Because of Christ's resurrection, we have hope. Hope that God is always with us. Hope for a better future, no matter what our present circumstances are. Hope that death itself has been defeated.

C. S. Lewis wrote about the hope of heaven in his book *Mere Christianity*, denying that such a hope is simply escapism or wishful thinking. Because Christians have hope, he said, they refuse to accept the world the way it is.

> If you read history you will find that the Christians who did most for the present world were just those who thought most of the next. The Apostles themselves, who set on foot the conversion of the Roman Empire, the great men who built up the Middle Ages, the English Evangelicals who abolished the Slave Trade, all left their mark on Earth, precisely because their minds were occupied with Heaven. It is since Christians have largely ceased to think of the other world that they have become so ineffective in this. Aim at Heaven, and you will get earth 'thrown in': aim at earth and you will get neither.[1]

For reflection . . .

Can you recall a time in your life when God replaced discouragement with hope?

How does Christ's resurrection, in general, and our own hope of heaven, in particular, give us powerful, overcoming hope?

Because of Jesus and his resurrection . . .

You Can Experience the Reality of the Cross

For the message of the cross is foolishness to those
who are perishing, but to us who are being
saved it is the power of God.
1 Corinthians 1:18

Jeffrey Ebert was five years old when he first learned the true meaning of love. He was sitting on his mother's lap, enjoying a late-night ride home in the family car. (This was before mandatory seatbelts and car seats.) Suddenly, a drunk driver traveling on the other side of the road lost control of his car, swerved, and hit the Eberts head-on. After the collision, Jeffrey woke up covered in blood.

Years later, writing about the crash in *Leadership* magazine, Jeffrey said, "Then I learned that the blood wasn't mine at all, but my mother's. In that split second when two headlights glared into her eyes, she instinctively pulled me closer to her chest and curled her body around mine. It was her body that slammed against the dashboard, her head that shattered the windshield. She took the impact of the collision so I didn't have to."[1]

Jeffrey's mother survived but was critically injured. He never forgot his mother's love, how she put herself in harm's way for him. Jeffrey Ebert would have been killed without his mother's sacrifice.

That's the message of the cross. *Jesus Christ loves us so much, he was willing to die—so that we could live.* The cross is a place of redemption and a place of relationship. Jesus told his disciples, "Greater love has no one than this: to lay down one's life for one's friends" (John 15:13).

In *The Green Mile,* a movie based on Stephen King's book of the same name, Tom Hanks plays Paul Edgecomb, head guard on death row at the Cold Mountain Prison. One day a new prisoner arrives. John Coffey, played by Michael Clarke Duncan, is a giant, close to seven feet tall. A quiet, gentle man, Coffey had been falsely convicted of murder.

Strangely, Coffey possesses a mysterious gift—he can heal people by literally absorbing their illnesses. Edgecomb suffers from a urinary tract infection, and with just one touch from Coffey, Edgecomb is cured.

When Edgecomb learns that the warden's wife, a dear friend, has an inoperable brain tumor, he and other guards sneak Coffey out of the prison on a midnight run to the warden's house. As the guards escort John into the house, they hear the warden's wife screaming in agony. Once a kind and loving woman, she had been reduced to a mere shell, driven mad with pain.

John slowly approaches the warden's wife. She asks his name, and he tells her, "John Coffey, ma'am. Just like the drink but not spelled the same." They talk for a few minutes, and then he leans over her. "I see it," he says. Suddenly John takes her hands and places his mouth near hers.

Black bugs, representing cancer, stream from her body into Coffey's. The room lights up, and the house shakes. Then, suddenly all becomes quiet. The warden's wife is completely changed: the disease had left her body, and she returned to normal. John Coffey, however, falls over and begins to cough loudly. He had taken her sickness upon himself.

The warden's wife was made whole—because John absorbed the pain. From the Bible's vantage point, that is precisely what Jesus did during his passion at Calvary. He took your pain upon himself and offers you the gifts of forgiveness, wholeness, and new life.

For reflection . . .

Take a moment to offer God thanks for sending his Son to suffer on the cross and for raising him from the dead, thereby providing for our forgiveness and new life.

chapter 26

Because of Jesus and his resurrection . . .

You Can Know God Personally

I consider everything a loss because of the surpassing worth of knowing Christ Jesus my Lord. Philippians 3:8

One Saturday morning, a pastor decided to visit some of his church members. When he arrived at one house, the pastor saw lights on and he heard sounds inside. It was clear that someone was home. But though he knocked several times, no one answered.

Before returning to his car, the pastor placed in the door his card, on which he had written a Bible verse, Revelation 3:20: "Behold, I stand at the door and knock. If anyone hears My voice and opens the door, I will come in to him and dine with him, and he with Me" (NKJV).

The next day at church, the pastor's card turned up in the offering plate. Below the pastor's message was written another Bible verse, Genesis 3:10: "I heard Your voice in the garden, and I was afraid because I was naked; and I hid myself" (NKJV).

These days many people are hiding from God. Only about 40 percent of Americans show up at church each week, even though surveys tell us that 90 percent of Americans believe in God and that many of those want to have a personal relationship with him.

Yet that is exactly why Jesus Christ came! He didn't come to launch a religious system, burdened with rules and regulations. He came so that everyone could have a thriving personal relationship with God through him. The central message of the Bible and the core reason for Christ's birth, death, and resurrection is this: *We were created to enjoy a personal relationship with God!*

Here are some of the things God offers us through a relationship with Jesus Christ:

Complete forgiveness—1 John 1:9

A clean slate and a fresh start—2 Corinthians 5:17

The gift of eternal life—John 3:16

Freedom from guilt—Romans 8:1

Freedom from fear—2 Timothy 1:7

God's power in our lives—Philippians 4:13

God's presence in our lives—Matthew 28:20

God's principles to live by—2 Timothy 3:16-17

God's people for encouragement—Hebrews 10:24-25

God's purpose for life—Colossians 1:28-29

More importantly, we can know that God cares for us and will never abandon us—no matter what happens.

In *Four Pillars of a Man's Heart,* Stu Weber tells of a family on vacation, relaxing at a house beside a beautiful lake. While the father puttered with something in the boathouse, his three-year-old son, Billy, was left to the care of his five-year-old sister and a twelve-year-old cousin. When the two older children became distracted as they played on the lawn, Billy wandered down to the lake to check out a shiny aluminum boat bobbing beside the dock. Stretching one foot toward the bobbing boat, Billy lost his balance and fell into the water.

The splash caught the attention of the twelve-year-old, who let loose a shriek that in turn brought Dad running. Realizing what had happened, he dove in the lake and began searching for the boy. But the water was so murky, he couldn't see. He came up for a quick gasp of air and plunged back under the water. In terrible panic, his only thought was to stretch out his arms and legs as far as possible in hope of feeling his son. Running out of oxygen, he started toward the surface for another breath.

But as he ascended, Dad felt little Billy, arms clutching a pier post some four feet underwater. After prying the boy's fingers loose, they exploded through the water's surface to gulp life-giving air.

Adrenaline still surging, Dad carried little Billy around, holding him close, unable to put him down. Finally, when heart rates returned to normal and nerves calmed somewhat, Dad asked his boy a question.

"Billy, what on earth were you *doing* down there, hanging onto that post so far underwater?"

"Just waitin' for you, Dad. Just waitin' for you!"[1]

Billy's reply, replete with all the wisdom of a child, reaches out and grabs our hearts. When you feel as if you can no longer hold on, release yourself into God's presence and care. He is faithful—and we *can* know him personally.

For reflection . . .

How has knowing God personally changed your life?

What kinds of things help you develop that relationship?

chapter 27

Because of Jesus and his resurrection . . .

You Can Receive Complete Forgiveness

"Jesus, remember me when you come into your kingdom." Luke 23:42

Jesus was dying. Nailed to the cross, his agony was inconceivable. Yet even in the last moments of his life, Jesus reached out with God's love and forgiveness. One of the criminals crucified next to him begged for forgiveness, and Jesus granted it immediately. "Today," he told the man, "you will be with me in paradise" (Luke 23:43).

In today's world, we seldom get much grace. Most of the time, our experience is like that of Dave Hagler, a former baseball umpire. Hagler was stopped for speeding one snowy day in Boulder, Colorado. In a *Los Angeles Times* article, Hagler said he tried without luck to talk the officer out of giving him a speeding ticket, arguing his insurance rates would go up. But the unsympathetic police officer told Hagler he should go to court and try to get the ticket reduced or thrown out there.

"The first game of the next baseball season," Hagler said, "I'm umpiring behind home plate—and the first batter up is the same policeman. I recognize him, he recognizes me. He asks me how the thing went with the ticket. I tell him, 'Swing at everything.'"[1]

Easter is God's invitation to experience grace, forgiveness, and a new start. How important is this? Paul said nothing is more important: "For what I received I passed on to you as of first importance: that Christ died for our sins according to the Scriptures, that he was buried, that he was raised on the third day according to the Scriptures" (1 Corinthians 15:3–4).

Living in a prison of resentment and regret, trapped by bitterness and paralyzed by past mistakes, is no way to live! Maybe you've felt that way. Maybe you've felt like Humpty Dumpty: "Nothing could put me back together again." You're wrong. God specializes in new beginnings. That's what Easter is all about. "If anyone is in Christ, the new creation has come: The old has gone, the new is here!" (2 Corinthians 5:17).

Many of us don't believe that God can forgive us. We stay trapped in the past. We can neither enjoy the present nor dream about the future. We are haunted by what might have been.

Are you holding on to a past hurt? Perhaps you failed, falling flat on your face, and are still haunted by the embarrassment. Maybe you were in an abusive relationship and still carry the scars. Maybe your parents or your spouse rejected you, and you can't believe that anyone would ever love you for who you are.

There's good news. God can set you free from the prison of resentment. He can heal you from the poison of regret. On Good Friday, Jesus took our pain and our failures, and he carried them to the cross. With his suffering and death, he wiped our slates clean. Then, on Easter, he stepped out of the grave and invited us to follow in his footsteps.

The book of Hebrews tells us that Jesus knows our weaknesses and failings, and yet he still accepts us. "We do not have a high priest who is unable to empathize with our weaknesses, but we have one who has been tempted in every way, just as we are—yet he did not sin. Let us then approach God's throne of grace with confidence, so that we may receive mercy and find grace to help us in our time of need" (Hebrews 4:15–16).

When we sin, when things go wrong, our first impulse is to hide *from God*. But because of Easter, we can run *to God*, and he will forgive us.

We don't need to be afraid of God. Jesus, who lived and died and rose again for our sakes, calls his followers his friends (John 15:15).

For reflection . . .

Are you living with the clean slate and fresh start that Jesus offers through his death and resurrection? Or do you feel trapped in the past?

Read Hebrews 4:15–16 again. What does that Scripture mean to you today?

chapter 28

Because of Jesus and his resurrection . . .

You Can Know That Death Is Defeated

> *Even though I walk through the valley of the shadow of death, I fear no evil, for You are with me; Your rod and Your staff, they comfort me.*
> Psalm 23:4, NASB

I heard a story of a woman caught in a frightening storm in the middle of the Atlantic. She kept all the children on the ship from panicking by telling them Bible stories. After reaching port safely, the ship's captain approached the woman and asked, "How in the world did you remain calm when everyone else was afraid the ship would sink?"

She said, "I have two daughters: one in New York, one in heaven. Either way, I knew I would see one of my daughters in a few hours, and it really didn't matter to me which one."

That's the type of calm confidence promised by Jesus Christ and available to every believer.

As a pastor, I've spoken at many funeral memorial services. I often share the following anecdote at those services:

> A couple in their eighties died in a car crash. They had been in good health because the wife had insisted on eating only health food and getting plenty of exercise.
>
> When they reached the pearly gates, Saint Peter took them to a mansion, decked out with a beautiful kitchen, master bedroom suite, and backyard jacuzzi.
>
> The husband told Saint Peter, "We love the house, but how much is it going to cost?"
>
> "It's free," Peter replied. "This is heaven."
>
> Next, they walked out back to see the championship golf course. They would have golfing privileges every day, and each week the course transformed into a new course, all putting the great golf courses on earth to shame.
>
> "What are the green fees?" the husband asked.
>
> "This is heaven," Peter said. "You play for free."
>
> Next, they went to the clubhouse, where they saw a lavish buffet, laid out with the cuisines of the world. "How much is it to eat here?" the old man asked.
>
> "Don't you understand yet?" Saint Peter asked. "This is heaven. It's free!"

"Well, where are the low-fat and low-choles-
terol foods?" the old man asked timidly.

"That's the best part," Peter explained. "You
can eat as much as you like, of whatever you like,
and never gain weight. This is heaven!"

The old man looked at his wife and said,
"You and your darned bran muffins! I could have
been here ten years ago!"

I'm not sure there are golf courses and all-you-can-eat
buffets in heaven. But that story captures an essential truth.
*God promises us eternal life through the death and resurrection
of his Son, Jesus.* Eternal life is better than anything we could
hope for or imagine. As Christians, we will live forever in the
joy of God's presence!

In *The Last Battle*, the final book in *The Chronicles of
Narnia* series, C. S. Lewis painted a picture of eternal life. At
the end of the book, the children learn they can't go back to
earth from the enchanted land of Narnia. They have died, the
great lion, Aslan, tells them. Now they can remain with him
forever.

"The term is over," he tells them. "The holidays have
begun. The dream is ended: this is the morning."

Rather than being filled with sorrow, the children's hearts
leap with exuberant hope.

And thus *The Chronicles of Narnia* concludes:

And as He spoke He no longer looked to them
like a lion; but the things that began to happen
after that were so great and beautiful that I cannot

write them. And for us this is the end of all the stories, and we can most truly say that they all lived happily ever after. But for them it was only the beginning of the real story. All their life in this world and all their adventures in Narnia had only been the cover and the title page: now at last they were beginning Chapter One of the Great Story which no one on earth has read: which goes on forever: in which every chapter is better than the one before.[1]

For reflection . . .

What did C. S. Lewis mean when he spoke of our earthly lives as only the cover and the title page of the real story?

How would your life be affected today if you focused on the anticipation of "the Great Story which no one on earth has read: which goes on forever: in which every chapter is better than the one before"?

Because of Jesus and his resurrection . . .

You Can Live with Eternal Values

For to me, to live is Christ and to die is gain.
Philippians 1:21

When Jesus wanted to make a point, he usually didn't give a lecture. Instead, he told a story, also known as a parable. Here's a parable for our time:

A police officer arrived at the scene of an accident before the dust had even settled. He found that a wealthy young man had been thrown out of his Mercedes just before it plunged over a steep cliff and crashed onto the rocks far below in a ball of flames. The young man was standing along the roadside at the top of the cliff, weeping. He was bleeding profusely from the stump of his shoulder, all that was left of his arm.

"My Mercedes! My Mercedes!" the young man howled.

"You ought to be thankful you're alive," the amazed officer said.

"But it had twenty thousand dollars worth of options," the man whimpered, staring down at the burning wreckage.

"There are things more important than that stupid car," the police officer insisted, guiding the injured man away from the cliff. "We've got to get you to a hospital. Your arm has been torn off, and you could bleed to death!"

The young man looked down and noticed for the first time that his arm was missing. Horrified, he screamed, "My Rolex! My Rolex!"

An exaggeration? Not by much. Today, countless news headlines tell stories of people who destroy their lives simply because they fear losing their material possessions. They murder to collect insurance policies, defraud to build business empires, and steal to accumulate what they cannot keep. They are willing to risk their lives to *gain things,* but fear prevents them from risking their things to gain *life.*

The resurrection shows us that everything that has no eternal value is eternally out of date. It's like building a nest in a tree that you know will be chopped down tomorrow. Here today, gone tomorrow.

Perhaps no one understood eternal values better than Giovanni Francesco Bernardone, better known in the English-speaking world as Saint Francis of Assisi. The son of a wealthy merchant, Francis hoped to follow his father into business and live a life of luxury. But, one day, while walking by a ruined church, he seemed to hear Jesus say, "Francis, repair my falling house." So, Francis sold some silk from his father's storehouse to pay for repairing the church. His father, however, thought it a waste of money and demanded that Francis come to his senses. When Francis refused, his father disowned him. Rather than walk away from God, Francis gave back all his possessions, even the clothes on his back.

Francis had too much to live on and not enough to live for. So, he gave it all up, restored the church, and became one of the most beloved Christians in history.

In his book *Death by Suburb,* David Goetz wrote, "Too much of the good life ends up being toxic, deforming us spiritually."[1] Rather than "the good life," Christ offers us a life full of meaning and purpose. Eugene Peterson described that well in his paraphrase of Jesus' words in Matthew 11:

> *Are you tired? Worn out? Burned out on religion? Come to me. Get away with me and you'll recover your life. I'll show you how to take a real rest. Walk with me and work with me—watch how I do it. Learn the unforced rhythms of grace. I won't lay anything heavy or ill-fitting on you. Keep company with me and you'll learn to live freely and lightly.*
> Matthew 11:28–30, *The Message*

C. S. Lewis reminded us in his essay "The Weight of Glory" that the only thing in this world that lasts forever is people—people, made in God's image, are meant to live forever. "There are no *ordinary* people," he wrote. "You have never talked to a mere mortal. Nations, cultures, arts, civilizations—these are mortal, and their life is to ours as the life of a gnat. But it is immortals whom we joke with, work with, marry, snub, and exploit—immortal horrors or everlasting splendors."[2]

Anything that is not eternal is eternally out of date.

For reflection . . .

Do you have too much to live on and not enough to live for?

How are you leveraging your life and resources for maximum eternal impact?

chapter 30

Because of Jesus and his resurrection . . .

You Can Know That Jesus Christ Is Alive

In their fright the women bowed down with their faces to the ground, but the men said to them, "Why do you look for the living among the dead? He is not here; he has risen!" Luke 24:5–6

Inspired by the Arizona Diamondbacks coming from behind to beat the New York Yankees in the 2001 World Series, the editors of *Sports Illustrated* put together a top-ten list of "famous comebacks." Elvis Presley made the list, as did Michael Jordan and Muhammad Ali. Harry Truman—who defeated Thomas Dewey in the 1948 presidential election, even though the *Chicago Tribune* declared Dewey the winner—made the list as well. Two countries, Japan and Germany, were on the list, as was "humanity" for surviving the Black Death, the plague that killed twenty-five million people in Europe during the fourteenth century.

Who was number one on the all-time comeback list? Jesus Christ. "Defies critics and stuns the Romans with his resurrection," the editors of *Sports Illustrated* wrote.[1]

Both before and after Jesus, there were many would-be messiahs, or deliverers, in Israel. The story was always the same. They would gather a few followers and start causing trouble. At some point, they would go too far and do something that caught the attention of the Romans. Then the Roman soldiers would come in and crush them, bringing a swift end to the false messiah and his followers. No one ever came back against the Romans.

Except for Jesus.

On Easter, the third day after he had been crucified, Jesus rose from the dead. And the movement the Romans believed they had crushed came back to life with him. Three hundred years later, the Roman emperor would bow down and worship Jesus Christ. Small wonder that Jesus' resurrection is considered the greatest comeback of all time. Nothing else comes close.

Some modern theologians think Christ's resurrection never happened. These theologians believe the early Christians were speaking metaphorically when they said Jesus rose from the dead. But that explanation doesn't add up.

In *Knowing the Truth about the Resurrection,* William Lane Craig recalls how a student friend of his once remarked, "There ain't gonna be no Easter this year."

"Why not?" Craig asked incredulously.

"They found the body," his friend replied.

Craig observes, "Despite his irreverent humor, my friend displayed a measure of insight often not shared by modern theologians. Many of them are perfectly willing to assert that Jesus died and rotted in the grave, but that the resurrection still has value as a symbol of 'newness of life' or 'new beginning,' so that Christianity can go on quite nicely as though nothing were changed. My friend's joke implied that without the resurrection Christianity is worthless."[2]

Craig goes on to state that the first Christians certainly would have agreed with his friend.[3] The apostle Paul told the Corinthian believers, "If Christ has not been raised, our preaching is useless and so is your faith" (1 Corinthians 15:14). Then he added, "If only for this life we have hope in Christ, we are of all people most to be pitied."

The truth is, two thousand years ago something caused the birth of a worldwide movement—a movement that turned the world upside down. The early church was fueled by the enthusiasm of people who one minute had been cowards about the future and days later were changing the future. The only explanation that fits? *They were witnesses to the reality of Jesus' resurrection. Jesus rose from the dead.*

In John 11, we read that Jesus heard that his friend Lazarus was ill. By the time Jesus arrived where Lazarus lived, however, it was too late. Jesus found Lazarus' sisters, Mary and Martha, in mourning; their brother was dead.

Jesus said a very strange thing to Martha: "I am the resurrection and the life. The one who believes in me will live, even though they die; and whoever lives by believing in me will never die." Then he asked her, "Do you believe this?" (John 11:25–26).

Martha said yes, and Jesus headed toward the grave where Lazarus was buried. After weeping for Lazarus, Jesus raised his friend from the dead.

"I am the resurrection and the life," Jesus said.

Do you believe this? That is the question of the ages!

For reflection . . .

How about you? Do you believe that Jesus is the resurrection and the life?

What would your spiritual condition be like if Jesus really wasn't raised from the dead and you had hope in Christ only for this life?

chapter 31

Because of Jesus and his resurrection . . .

You Can Be Resurrected Too

*Listen, I tell you a mystery: We will not all
sleep, but we will all be changed—in a flash,
in the twinkling of an eye, at the last trumpet.
For the trumpet will sound, the dead will be
raised imperishable, and we will be changed.
For the perishable must clothe itself with the
imperishable, and the mortal with immortality.*
1 Corinthians 15:51–53

I recently preached a two-sermon overview of the
book of Revelation. People tend to associate the book of
Revelation with the antichrist and with signs and beasts
and such. But as I told the folks at Bayside Church, the
book of Revelation isn't about figuring out what Russia
is going to do or who the antichrist is or when Christ is
coming back.

The believers who first read Revelation were suffering
intense persecution from the Roman Empire. Here's what
the book of Revelation is really about: Yes, life is tough; but

in the midst of life being tough, God ultimately has unbelievably great days ahead. No matter how bad things look or get, God is in control of all future events.

Although much of Revelation is filled with bad news and tribulation, shouts of praise spring up repeatedly. The current circumstances of John's readers were terrible; yet every time they caught a glimpse of the future, their discouragement was replaced with these sudden bursts of hope and joy.

And then the whole mood of Revelation changes in the last few chapters. Check out Revelation 21:1–5:

> *Then I saw "a new heaven and a new earth," for the first heaven and the first earth had passed away, and there was no longer any sea. I saw the Holy City, the new Jerusalem, coming down out of heaven from God, prepared as a bride beautifully dressed for her husband. And I heard a loud voice from the throne saying, "Look! God's dwelling place is now among the people, and he will dwell with them. They will be his people, and God himself will be with them and be their God. 'He will wipe every tear from their eyes. There will be no more death' or mourning or crying or pain, for the old order of things has passed away."*
>
> *He who was seated on the throne said, "I am making everything new!"*

The Bible devotes much less space to describe eternity than it does to convince people that eternal life is available as a free gift from God. Most of the brief descriptions of eternity would more accurately be called hints, since they use terms and ideas from present experience to describe what we cannot fully grasp until we ourselves are there. These references hint at aspects of what our future will be like if we have accepted Christ's gift of eternal life.

Nonetheless, in regard to a Christian's future state, the New Testament does make two clear points, though at first these points can seem contradictory.

First, when a believer dies, there is no period of limbo or soul sleep. Jesus assured the repentant criminal hanging on the cross next to him: "Today you will be with me in paradise" (Luke 23:43). The apostle Paul spoke for all believers when he said that we "would prefer to be away from the body and at home with the Lord" (2 Corinthians 5:8). And as Paul, while imprisoned in Rome, shared with his good friends at Philippi, living would bring him opportunities to serve Christ and others, but his heart's desire was "to depart and be with Christ, which is better by far" (Philippians 1:23).

Second, a future day of resurrection will occur in conjunction with Christ's second coming. Paul described this incredible event in 1 Thessalonians 4:13–18:

> *Brothers and sisters, we do not want you to be uninformed about those who sleep in death, so that you do not grieve like the rest of mankind, who have no hope. For we believe that Jesus died and rose again, and so we believe that God will bring with Jesus those who have fallen asleep in him. According to the Lord's word, we tell you that we who are still*

> *alive, who are left until the coming of the Lord,*
> *will certainly not precede those who have fallen*
> *asleep. For the Lord himself will come down from*
> *heaven, with a loud command, with the voice of the*
> *archangel and with the trumpet call of God, and*
> *the dead in Christ will rise first. After that, we who*
> *are still alive and are left will be caught up together*
> *with them in the clouds to meet the Lord in the air.*
> *And so we will be with the Lord forever. Therefore*
> *encourage one another with these words.*

We aren't told much about the kind of existence believers have in the interim preceding this future resurrection (though we know that being in our Lord's presence will be awesome). Neither are we told much about what our state will be like after the resurrection. But think about this: "Our citizenship is in heaven," Paul wrote. "And we eagerly await a Savior from there, the Lord Jesus Christ, who, by the power that enables him to bring everything under his control, will transform our lowly bodies so that they will be like his glorious body" (Philippians 3:20–21).

Our resurrected bodies will be like Christ's glorious body. I'll tell you what: in my case, and probably in your case too, that's a significant upgrade!

The primary purpose of the book of Revelation wasn't to give a chronology of future events; neither was that the primary purpose of Paul's words to the Thessalonians regarding the second coming of Christ. He immediately went on to say, "Now, brothers and sisters, about times and dates we do not need to write to you, for you know very well that the day of the Lord will come like a thief in the night" (1 Thessalonians 5:1–2).

Paul had two critical messages to communicate. First, rather than being surprised by future events, Christ-followers should be awake, alert, and self-controlled (1 Thessalonians 5:4–8). Second, we should "encourage one another" and "build each other up" (4:18; 5:11) with the promise of Christ's return and our own resurrection.

I can't think of a better way to end this final chapter on the benefits of Jesus' resurrection. Be encouraged, brothers and sisters in Christ. *Because Jesus died and rose again, so we too will be resurrected!*

Maranatha! "Amen. Come, Lord Jesus" (Revelation 22:20)!

For reflection . . .

How can the Bible's perspective about the future help us when we face hard times now?

How does it make you feel to know that God's grand plan is to transform the "lowly bodies" of believers so that they will be like Christ's "glorious body"? Spend some time thanking the Lord for the promise of your own future resurrection.

chapter 32

Evidence for the Resurrection

*If Christ has not been raised, our preaching is
useless and so is your faith.*
1 Corinthians 15:14

*Christianity does not hold the resurrection to
be one among many tenets of belief. Without
faith in the resurrection there would be no
Christianity at all. The Christian church would
never have begun; the Jesus-movement would
have fizzled out. . . . Christianity stands or falls
with the truth of the resurrection. Once disprove
it, and you have disposed of Christianity.*
Michael Green[1]

As I mentioned in the introduction to this book, I grew
up in a family of skeptics. When it came to Christianity's
greatest claim, the resurrection of Jesus, I had serious
doubts. I was skeptical about stories claiming that a dead
man had come back to life. I was skeptical about claims
that the tomb was actually empty that Easter morning.

I was skeptical that accounts were credible of people who claimed to encounter a risen Christ. I was impressed by the sincerity of Christians who believed he rose from the dead, but I was convinced they were sincerely misguided.

If these doubts sound familiar, then read on. The following pages detail the evidence that replaced my skepticism with confident faith.

A Brief History

In AD 66, the Jews, outraged that the Roman governor Florus had been stealing from the temple in Jerusalem, rebelled against the Roman Empire. Led by guerilla captains such as Simon bar-Giora, whom some thought could be the Messiah, they defeated the Roman garrison in Jerusalem. When the Roman governor of Syria, Cestius Gallus, sent in reinforcements, they were defeated as well. Tens of thousands joined the rebel army. It seemed God would finally deliver Israel from the Roman occupation.

Four years later, however, Jerusalem lay in ruins following a several-month siege. The temple was destroyed. As many as one million Jews died or were carried off into slavery during the Great Revolt against Rome. The revolution was crushed. Simon bar-Giora and other rebels were taken to Rome, where they were paraded in front of crowds and then put to death.

Now suppose, says N. T. Wright, a leading New Testament scholar, that a few followers of Simon, hiding from the Roman army, went around saying that Simon really was the Messiah. Then suppose that, despite all the evidence, they claimed that

Simon, and not the Roman emperor, was lord of the whole world. Anyone who heard them would think they had lost their minds. Wright observes, "The verdict of madness, of a kind of criminal lunacy which turns reality upside down and inside out, seems inevitable."[2]

Yet that is exactly what the followers of Jesus did. After Jesus was crucified, his followers began preaching that he was the Messiah (which is the same as *Christ* from Greek), the lord of the world, and the Son of God. But instead of calling them mad, thousands of people believed the disciples.

Why? Because the disciples claimed that Jesus had risen from the dead. They testified that they had been to Jesus' tomb and saw it was empty. Jesus had appeared to them, walked with them, and even eaten with them. Then he had sent them out to tell the whole world that he was the Son of God.

Without this claim that Jesus rose from the dead, Wright argues in his 780-page book, *The Resurrection of the Son of God,* there is no Christianity. Either the disciples were telling the truth, or they were mad. For nearly two thousand years, the testimony to the resurrection of Jesus Christ has forced people to choose one of these two alternatives.

Throughout the centuries, Christians have held the position that there is plenty of evidence to convince rational, unbiased people that Jesus did, in fact, rise from the dead. Is this still true today? Can a twenty-first century American believe that the resurrection really happened?

Eyewitness Testimonies

One early Christian statement about the resurrection is found in 1 Corinthians, where the apostle Paul repeats an early creed (or statement of faith) of the church:

> For what I received I passed on to you as of first importance: that Christ died for our sins according to the Scriptures, that he was buried, that he was raised on the third day according to the Scriptures, and that he appeared to Cephas, and then to the Twelve. After that, he appeared to more than five hundred of the brothers and sisters at the same time, most of whom are still living, though some have fallen asleep. 1 Corinthians 15:3–6

In his book *The Case for Christ,* Lee Strobel interviewed New Testament scholar Craig Blomberg, who pointed out that Paul was converted and met Ananias and some other disciples in Damascus within about two years of the resurrection; and he met with Peter and the other apostles in Jerusalem within about five years of the resurrection. Paul heard testimony from eyewitnesses who summarized their faith using this statement—Jesus was crucified, buried, and resurrected. Blomberg stated that modern scholars who argue that the resurrection was a myth, invented decades after Jesus' death, ignore this crucial piece of evidence.[3]

Paul himself says this in 1 Corinthians 15:

- The resurrection of Jesus did not happen in secret.

- Jesus was seen by large numbers of people in different locations, at different times, and in different circumstances over a forty-day period.

- Most of the people who saw Jesus were still alive when Paul was writing, so his testimony could be verified.

The Accuracy of the New Testament

The late F. F. Bruce, who was a New Testament scholar at the University of Manchester, stated, "The evidence for our New Testament writings is ever so much greater than the evidence for many writings of classical authors, the authenticity of which no one dreams of questioning. And if the New Testament were a collection of secular writings, their authenticity would generally be regarded as beyond all doubt."[4]

As an example, Craig Blomberg notes that although the earliest biographies of Alexander the Great were written more than four hundred years after his death, historians still regard them to be generally trustworthy. The earliest accounts of Jesus' life, by comparison, were likely written within thirty years of his death. "Historically speaking, especially compared with Alexander the Great," Blomberg says, "that's like a news flash!"[5]

Josh McDowell, who spent years trying to disprove the New Testament, finally accepted it as historically accurate—in part because so many ancient copies of it exist. "If one discards the Bible as being unreliable," he wrote in *The New Evidence*

That Demands a Verdict, "then one must discard almost all literature of antiquity."[6]

The Alternative Theories Don't Hold Up

For nearly two thousand years, skeptics have come up with ways to explain away the resurrection and the empty tomb. But under close examination, not one of these alternatives holds up.

Alternative 1: Jesus Did Not Really Die

This alternative speculates that Jesus didn't actually die on the cross. Instead, shock from the loss of blood during the crucifixion and from the beating Jesus endured earlier sent him into a coma. When Jesus was placed in the tomb, the coolness of the stone and the aroma of the burial spices revived him. When he came out of the grave, the disciples assumed he had been resurrected.

But when examined closely, this theory falls apart. First, the Romans crucified thousands of people. As the film *The Passion of the Christ* illustrates, Roman soldiers were brutal, efficient, and merciless when it came to crucifixion. They would not be fooled by a coma caused by loss of blood. They had a vested interest in making sure Jesus was dead.

The account of Jesus' death in the gospel of John included this detail: a Roman soldier thrust a spear into Jesus' side, and a gush of water and blood came out (John 19:34). Modern medicine explains this detail: the spear pierced the pericardium, the covering of the heart. When a person dies, the pericardium fills with a clear fluid. The spear went through the pericardium and into the heart, causing a flow of water and blood.

Alternative 2: The Stolen Body Theory

This alternative argues that the disciples, or someone else, stole the body.

But who had the means and the motive to steal the body? Not the Romans or the Jewish authorities—they wanted Jesus dead. Had they taken the body, they could have produced it and then snuffed out the Christian church in its infancy. Even the disciples seemed to be unlikely suspects. They would have been little match for the Roman guards at the tomb. Also, they had little to gain by lying about the missing body. Put yourself in their shoes: "OK, we're going to steal the body. And then we're going to lie and claim the body was resurrected. Then, we're going to have the unspeakable privilege of living as penniless evangelists, wandering around for the rest of our lives being beaten, thrown in jail, and put to death." (Anyone reading this want to sign up?)

According to tradition, all of the disciples except John were put to death, many by crucifixion, for testifying that Jesus had risen from the grave. People will die for their faith if they believe that its claims are true. But people will not die for their faith if they know that its claims are false.

Alternative 3: The Wrong Tomb Theory

Another popular theory contends that the women, distraught and overcome by grief, missed their way in the darkness of the early morning and went to the wrong tomb. In their distress, they *imagined* Christ had risen, since the tomb was empty.

This theory, however, fails before the same fact that eliminates the previous one. If the women went to the wrong tomb, why didn't the Jewish religious leaders go to the right tomb and produce the body? Furthermore, it is inconceivable that all of Jesus' followers would succumb to the same mistake. And certainly Joseph of Arimathea, owner of the tomb, would have solved the problem. In addition, it must be remembered that this was a private burial ground, not a public cemetery. There was no other tomb nearby that would have allowed them to make this mistake.

Alternative 4: The Hallucination Theory

This theory argues that the disciples wanted to see Jesus so badly that they imagined he rose from the grave. In essence, they had a hallucination in which they saw Jesus.

This theory, however, also fails under scrutiny. For one, hallucinations are not group events. A psychologist has noted that five hundred different people having the same hallucination at exactly the same time would be a greater miracle than the resurrection itself.

The Transformation of the Disciples

One of the greatest proofs of the resurrection is the existence of the church. There were many would-be messiahs, both before and after Jesus. The Romans arrested them, killed them, and in doing so crushed their followers. All of these so-called messiahs stayed dead. Their followers disappeared.

For a while, that's what everyone, including the disciples, thought would happen with Jesus. The disciples weren't expecting the resurrection. After Jesus' death, they scattered. They were crushed. They hid in an upper room in Jerusalem and waited for their doom.

After the resurrection, the disciples were transformed. In Acts 2:22–24, Peter, who earlier had denied Jesus because he was afraid of a servant girl, proclaimed to thousands that Jesus had come back from the dead. "Fellow Israelites, listen to this," he said. "Jesus of Nazareth was a man accredited by God to you by miracles, wonders and signs, which God did among you through him, as you yourselves know. This man was handed over to you by God's deliberate plan and foreknowledge; and you, with the help of wicked men, put him to death by nailing him to the cross. But God raised him from the dead, freeing him from the agony of death, because it was impossible for death to keep its hold on him."

In response, no one said, "I don't know what this fellow is talking about; I never saw any signs or miracles." No one said, "I've never heard of Jesus." Instead, history shows that three thousand people responded by becoming followers of

Jesus Christ. They knew Peter spoke the truth. They knew the reality of Jesus' death and resurrection and why those things had taken place in their midst.

As John R. W. Stott said, "Perhaps the transformation of the disciples of Jesus is the greatest evidence of all for the resurrection, because it is entirely uncontrived."[7]

What was it that changed a band of frightened, cowardly disciples into men of courage and conviction? What was it that changed Peter? What was it that enabled Peter to risk his life by saying he had seen Jesus risen from the dead? What was it that changed Thomas' doubt and skepticism into a confident faith?

There's only one answer: Jesus Christ did indeed rise from the dead!

The Evidence of Fulfilled Prophecy

During my years of skepticism, the evidence of fulfilled prophecy proved most troublesome. I realized I had no answer when faced with the scores of Old Testament predictions that had been fulfilled, all of them written hundreds of years before Christ's time!

Here are some of the prophecies about Jesus' death and resurrection that were fulfilled:

- He would ride into Jerusalem on a donkey.
  —Zechariah 9:9; John 12:13–14
- He would enter the temple.
  —Malachi 3:1; Matthew 21:12–13

- He would be betrayed by a friend.
  —Psalm 41:9; Matthew 26:50
- He would be sold for thirty pieces of silver.
  —Zechariah 11:12; Matthew 26:15
- The silver would be thrown into the temple.
  – Zechariah 11:13; Matthew 27:5
- The silver would be used to buy the potter's field.
  – Zechariah 11:13; Matthew 27:6–7
- He would be arrested as a criminal.
  – Isaiah 53:12; Luke 22:37
- He would be forsaken by his disciples.
  – Zechariah 13:7; Matthew 26:31, 56
- He would be accused by false witnesses.
  – Psalm 35:11; Matthew 26:60–61
- He would remain silent before his accusers.
  – Isaiah 53:7; Matthew 26:62–63
- He would be wounded and beaten.
  – Isaiah 53:5; John 19:1–3
- He would be whipped and spat upon.
  – Isaiah 50:6; Mark 14:65
- He would be mocked.
  – Psalm 22:7–8; Matthew 27:39–40
- His hands and feet would be pierced.
  – Psalm 22:16; John 20:27
- People would shake their heads at him.
  – Psalm 109:25; Matthew 27:39
- His clothes would be divided and lots cast for them.
  – Psalm 22:18; Mark 15:24

- He would be offered gall and vinegar to drink.
  – Psalm 69:21; John 19:29
- Not one of his bones would be broken.
  – Psalm 34:20; John 19:33
- His side would be pierced.
  – Zechariah 12:10; John 19:34
- Darkness would fall in broad daylight.
  – Amos 8:9; Matthew 27:45
- He would be buried in a rich man's tomb.
  – Isaiah 53:9; Matthew 27:57–60
- He would be resurrected from thes dead.
  – Psalm 16:10; 30:3; 118:17; Hosea 6:2; Matthew 28:9

Josh McDowell notes that Peter Stoner, in his book *Science Speaks* (Moody Press, 1963), applied the science of probability to just eight prophecies regarding Christ. Stoner asserted that the odds any man could have fulfilled all eight prophecies are 1 in 10^{17}. That would be 1 in 100,000,000,000,000,000. To illustrate this staggering possibility, Stoner suggested the following scenario:

> Take 10 to the 17th silver dollars and lay them on the face of Texas. They will cover all of the state two feet deep. Now mark one of these silver dollars and stir the whole mass thoroughly, all over the state. Blindfold a man and tell him that he can travel as far as he wishes, but he must pick up one silver dollar and say that this is the right one. What chance would he have of getting the right one? Just the same chance that the prophets

would have had of writing these eight prophecies and having them all come true in any one man, from their day to the present time, providing they wrote them according to their own wisdom.[8]

Lunatic, Liar, or Lord

Almost two thousand years after Jesus' death and resurrection, it's become common to say that Jesus was a great man or a great moral teacher. But most of the people who make that claim have probably never carefully read the words Jesus spoke. Jesus claimed to speak for God. He said he could forgive sin. He called God his father. He said he was the Son of Man, another name for the Messiah. He told the people of Israel, who thought God belonged to them, that God loves all people.

But his most outrageous claim was this: Jesus predicted that he would be arrested and killed—and then, on the third day, he would "be raised to life" (Luke 9:22). These aren't merely the words of a great man or a great teacher. These are the words of someone who thinks he's the Son of God.

C. S. Lewis put it this way:

> A man who was merely a man and said the sort of things Jesus said would not be a great moral teacher. He would either be a lunatic—on a level with the man who says he is a poached egg—or else he would be the Devil of Hell. You must take your choice. Either this was, and is, the Son of God: or else a madman or something worse. You

can shut Him up for a fool, you can spit at Him and kill Him as a demon; or you can fall at His feet and call Him Lord and God. But let us not come with any patronizing nonsense about His being a great human teacher. He has not left that open to us. He did not intend to.[9]

Years ago, after finally approaching the evidence for Jesus' resurrection with an open mind, I discovered to my surprise that I agreed with Canon B. F. Westcott from Cambridge University, who stated: "Indeed, taking all the evidence together, it is not too much to say there is no historic incident better or more variously supported than the resurrection of Christ. Nothing but the antecedent assumption that it must be false could have suggested the idea of deficiency in the proof of it."[10]

Now, what about you? We have looked at what unleashing the power of Christ's resurrection can mean in our lives. If this book has helped you discover the reality of that resurrection, and you prayed the same prayer that changed the course of my life, congratulations! This could be the first day of the best of your life.

Or perhaps you're still skeptical. So was I—for a long time. I encourage you to keep reading, researching, and praying. Ask God to reveal himself to you. Put this in high gear. A lot is riding on this decision. If the resurrection is true—and the evidence is compelling—then you can experience God's forgiveness for your past, God's power for your present, and God's promises for your future. Why would you want to live any other way?

About the Author

Speaking Engagements

Ray Johnston is available to speak at churches and conferences. Please contact his assistant, Donna Bostwick, at DonnaB@baysideonline.com.

Thrive Conferences

Bayside Church is home to the annual Thrive Conference—for anyone who would like to be renewed, refreshed, and recharged for service through an upbeat, worshipful three-day conference. Please visit www.thriveconference.org for details.

Suggested Reading

I serve as a pastor of a church for people who usually don't like church. In the last sixteen years, we've seen thousands of people move from skepticism to Christianity. In conversations with former skeptics who have crossed the line of faith, many report that the following books have been helpful:

Did Jesus Rise from the Dead?
    Gary R. Habermas, Antony G. N. Flew, and Terry L. Miethe (Wipf & Stock, 2003)

Who Moved the Stone?
    Frank Morison (Zondervan, 1987)

The Case for Christ
    Lee Strobel (Zondervan, 1998)

The Case for Faith
    Lee Strobel (Zondervan, 2000)

The Case for Easter
    Lee Strobel (Zondervan, 2004)

Evidence That Demands a Verdict
Josh McDowell (Thomas Nelson, 1999)

A Ready Defense
Josh McDowell (Thomas Nelson, 1992)

More Than a Carpenter
Josh McDowell and Sean McDowell (Living Books, 2009)

Letters from a Skeptic
Gregory A. Boyd and Edward K. Boyd (David C. Cook, 2008)

The New Testament Documents: Are They Reliable?
F. F. Bruce (Wilder Publications, 2009)

The Reality of the Resurrection
Merrill C. Tenney (Moody, 1972)

Notes

Chapter 1: You Can Develop a Confident Faith

1. George Bernard Shaw, "Too True to Be Good," (New York: Samuel French, Inc., 1933), 99.

Chapter 4: You Can Discover That You Matter to God

1. René Schlaepfer, "HOPE-FULLY, a Hope Experience at Friends Church: Day 16: Who Am I?" Friends Church, Citrus Heights, CA, website, http://www.hope-fully.com/day-16---who-am-i.html; "The Dave Roever Story," Roever and Associates website, http://daveroever.org/roeverstory.php.

Chapter 5: You Can Experience Complete Transformation

1. "Ficks Reed, a Featured Furniture Provider in Upcoming Back-to-Back Episodes of 'Extreme Makeover: Home Edition,'" March 15, 2007, Ficks Reed website, http://www.ficksreed.com/FicksReedArticle.aspx?Id=3.
2. John Maxwell, *Thinking for a Change: Eleven Ways Highly Successful People Approach Life and Work* (New York: Warner Books, 2003), 27–33.

Chapter 7: You Can Trust the Bible

1. Josh McDowell, *The New Evidence That Demands a Verdict* (Nashville: Thomas Nelson, 1999), 68.
2. Bernard Ramm, *Protestant Christian Evidences* (Chicago: Moody Press, 1953), 232–33.

Chapter 9: You Can Live with a Sense of Wonder

1. Robert Fulghum, *All I Really Need to Know I Learned in Kindergarten* (New York: Random House, 1988).
2. Robert Fulghum, *Uh-Oh: Some Observations from Both Sides of the Refrigerator Door* (New York: Random House, 1991), 228.
3. Ibid.
4. Ibid., 228–29.

5. Diane Disney Miller, as told to Pete Martin, "My Dad, Walt Disney," *The Saturday Evening Post,* November 17, 1956, available at The Disney Archives and Mysteries blog, http://marciodisneyarchives. blogspot.com/2010/08/my-dad-walt-disney-by-diane-disney.html.

Chapter 11: You Can Live with God's Purpose
1. Mark Twain, *Mark Twain's Own Autobiography: The Chapters from the North American Review,* with an introduction and notes by Michael J. Kiskis (Madison: University of Wisconsin Press, 1990), 28.
2. George Bernard Shaw, "Epistle Dedicatory to Arthur Bingham Walkley," in *Man and Superman* (Cambridge, MA: The University Press, 1903), 29.

Chapter 12: You Can Know God
1. "Don v. Devil," *Time,* September 8, 1947, http://www.time.com/time/magazine/article/0,9171,804196-1,00.html.

Chapter 15: You Can Overcome Discouragement
1. Rick Warren, "What Do You Do When You Get Discouraged?" *Ministry Toolbox* newsletter no. 55 (June 12, 2002); Rick Warren, "Some Cures for Discouragement," *Ministry Toolbox* newsletter no. 121 (September 24, 2003); Rick Warren, "Is It Time for You to Take a Nap?" *Ministry Toolbox* newsletter no. 129 (November 19, 2003).

Chapter 17: You Can Trust God's Promises
1. Harold Kushner, *When All You've Ever Wanted Isn't Enough: The Search for a Life That Matters* (New York: Simon & Schuster, 1986), 165–66.

Chapter 19: You Can Experience God's Presence
1. Bob Smietana, "A Brother's Gift of Life," *The Covenant Companion,* September 2005, 28–30.

Chapter 20: You Can Stop Worrying
1. Warren W. Wiersbe, *The Wiersbe Bible Commentary: New Testament* (Colorado Springs: David C. Cook, 2007), 24.

Chapter 22: You Can Experience Real Peace
1. Mary Taylor Previte, *Hungry Ghosts: One Woman's Mission to Change Their World* (Grand Rapids: Zondervan, 1994), 20–21.

Chapter 23: You Can Expect Great Things from God
1. Donald J. Albers and Constance Reid, "An Interview of George B. Dantzig: The Father of Linear Programming," *College Mathematics Journal* 17, no. 4 (1986): 293–314.

Chapter 24: You Can Experience Hope

1. C. S. Lewis, *Mere Christianity* (New York: Touchstone, 1996), 119.

Chapter 25: You Can Experience the Reality of the Cross

1. Jeffrey Ebert, "Blood's Price," *Leadership*, Summer 1992, 46.

Chapter 26: You Can Know God Personally

1. Stu Weber, *Four Pillars of a Man's Heart: Bringing Strength into Balance* (Colorado Springs: Multnomah, 1997), 57.

Chapter 27: You Can Receive Complete Forgiveness

1. Harley Tinkham, "When It Comes to Blind Justice, Umpire's Sight Is Always 20/20," *Los Angeles Times,* March 4, 1990, http://articles. latimes.com/1990-03-04/sports/sp-2637_1_joe-morgan.

Chapter 28: You Can Know That Death Is Defeated

1. C. S. Lewis, *The Last Battle,* collector's edition (New York: HarperCollins, 2000), 210–11.

Chapter 29: You Can Live with Eternal Values

1. David L. Goetz, *Death by Suburb: How to Keep the Suburbs from Killing Your Soul* (New York: HarperCollins, 2006), 9.
2. C. S. Lewis, *The Weight of Glory: And Other Addresses* (New York: HarperCollins, 2001), 46.

Chapter 30: You Can Know That Jesus Christ Is Alive

1. "Bouncing Back Big-time," *Sports Illustrated,* November 12, 2001, http://sportsillustrated.cnn.com/vault/article/magazine/MAG1024225/ index.htm.
2. William Lane Craig, *Knowing the Truth about the Resurrection: Our Response to the Empty Tomb* (Ann Arbor, MI: Servant Books, 1988), 125.
3. Ibid.

Chapter 32: Evidence for the Resurrection

1. Michael Green, *Man Alive* (London: InterVarsity, 1967), 55.
2. N. T. Wright, *The Resurrection of the Son of God* (Minneapolis: Fortress, 2003), 558–59.
3. Lee Strobel, *The Case for Christ: A Journalist's Personal Investigation of the Evidence for Jesus* (Grand Rapids: Zondervan, 1998), 43–44.
4. F. F. Bruce, *The New Testament Documents: Are They Reliable?* (Grand Rapids: Eerdmans, and Downers Grove, IL: InterVarsity, 2003), 10.
5. Strobel, *The Case for Christ,* 40–42.

6. Josh McDowell, *The New Evidence That Demands a Verdict* (Nashville: Thomas Nelson, 1999), 68.

7. John R. W. Stott, *Basic Christianity,* 50th anniversary edition (Downers Grove, IL: InterVarsity), 70.

8. McDowell, *New Evidence That Demands a Verdict*, 193.

9. C. S. Lewis, *Mere Christianity* (New York: Touchstone, 1996), 56.

10. B. F. Westcott, *The Gospel of the Resurrection,* 4th ed (London, 1879), 4–6; quoted in Paul E. Little, *Know Why You Believe* (Downers Grove, IL: InterVarsity, 1988), 58.

Also Available

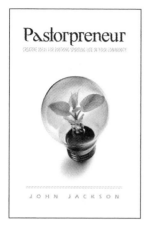

Pastorpreneur equips pastors to employ businesslike strategic planning and innovation skills to enhance their congregational leadership. Jackson's practical strategies and grand vision will empower you to explore new methods for maximum impact on your church and community . . . and become the church that you and God dreamed of.

Paperback, 192 pages, 5.5 x 8.5
ISBN: 978-1-60657-106-4
Retail: $15.99

Available for purchase at book retailers everywhere.

Learning about where you fit in the family of God can be experienced both in relationships with others and in personal reflection. *Finding Your Place in God's Plan* provides teaching, daily devotionals, and small group materials for these purposes.

Paperback, 176 pages, 5.5 x 8.5
ISBN: 978-1-60657-083-8
Retail: $15.99

Available for purchase at book retailers everywhere.

Also Available

This how-to for church growth outlines principles of growth for all sizes of congregations, while emphasizing that church growth is not about numbers, but about fulfilling God's vision for your church's impact on the world.

Paperback, 176 pages, 5.5 x 8.5
ISBN: 978-1-60657-107-1
Retail: $15.99

Available for purchase at book retailers everywhere.

Faith Has Its Reasons is a study of four different models of how apologetics should be done, an assessment of their strengths and weaknesses, and a proposal for integrating the best insights of each.

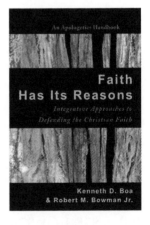

Paperback, 608 pages, 6 x 9
ISBN: 978-1-93280-534-5
Retail: $29.99

Available for purchase at book retailers everywhere.